Digging Out

Digging Out

A Practical Guide to Getting Out of Debt
and Paving the Path to a Secure Financial Future

Jodee Brydges

ABOOKS

Alive Book Publishing

Digging Out: A Practical Guide to Getting Out of Debt and Paving the
Path to a Secure Financial Future
Copyright © 2018 by Jodee Brydges

Cover Design and Illustrations by Michelle Fairbanks
Interior Book Design by Alex Johnson

ISBN 13: 978-1-63132-049-1
ISBN 10: 1-63132-049-1

Library of Congress Control Number: 2018947985
Library of Congress Cataloging-in-Publication Data
is available upon request. ·

First Edition

Published in the United States of America by ALIVE Book Publishing
and ALIVE Publishing Group, imprints of Advanced Publishing LLC
3200 A Danville Blvd., Suite 204, Alamo, California 94507
alivebookpublishing.com

PRINTED IN THE UNITED STATES OF AMERICA

10 9 8 7 6 5 4 3 2 1

Acknowledgments

This book would not have happened without the incredible support of my husband, Robert, my daughter, Chloe, my personal coach, David Speechly, and the encouragement and support from my dear family and friends who continued to cheer me on to the finish line. I am forever grateful to each and every one of you and thankful for your believing in me and my vision with this book.

I am so incredibly blessed for my dear friend Esme Tarder, who planted the seed for this book many years ago and encouraged me to write it. I also thank Esme for giving me the courage to face my own personal debt and determine the plan that was needed to "dig out." Furthermore, I am thankful and blessed to have and continue to have the opportunity to work with so many wonderful clients, industry leaders, employees of corporations, and to coach them on how to dig out and live the financial dreams they deserve.

Behind the scenes, a huge heartfelt thank you to my amazing editor, Jodi Brandon, who kept us on track, encouraged changes that improved the content of the book, and delivered quality feedback and edits. Additionally, many thanks to my logo and cover designer, Michelle Fairbanks, and my publisher, Eric Johnson, Alive Book Publishing. Eric and his team were amazing to work with, and it is an honor and privilege to be an ongoing contributing writer for his *Alive* magazine.

Lastly, thank you to my mom, who demonstrated an incredible work ethic throughout my life. That lesson gave me the perseverance to keep pushing to achieve this dream!

Contents

Introduction

Dig In and Learn How to Dig Out of Debt

If you want to be successful, find someone who has achieved the results you want and copy what they do and you'll achieve the same results.

— Tony Robbins

If you have picked up this book, you have done so for a good reason: YOU ARE IN DEBT! Credit card debt is once again on a rapid rise, has hit an all-time high, and surpassed the record set in 2008. According to a January 2018 *USA Today* article: "Revolving credit, mostly credit cards, increased by $11.2 billion to **$1.023 trillion,** according to the Federal Reserve. That nudged the figure past the $1.021 trillion high-water mark reached in April 2008, just before the housing and credit bubbles burst."[1]

Couple that with the rising mountain of student loan debt, which has climbed to an all-time record of $1.4 trillion, and it is apparent that a debt epidemic is spreading in the financial lives of individuals at all income levels.

According to a February 2018 *Time* article:
- More than 40 million Americans have student debt.
- 5.9 million owe more than $50,000.
- Americans combined have $1.4 trillion in outstanding student loans.

$1.023 trillion in credit card debt and $1.4 trillion in student loan debt seem like outrageous figures that can be hard to comprehend. Let's pause for a second and visualize 1 trillion dollars stacked in $100 bills.

In an interview on NPR in February 2008, author David Schwartz stated that "a trillion dollars stacked in $100 bills covers about 789 miles or 144 Mount Everests stacked on top of each other!" Add the student loan debt, and approximately 345 Mount Everests would be stacked on top of each other.[3] Talk about mountains of debt that Americans are racking up!

So, what does that mean to you? Breaking that large amount down into smaller figures, the average household's credit card debt is $8,600, according to a March 2018 article on Wallethub,[4] and the average debt per student borrower is $27,975, according to a March 2018 article on Studentloans.net.[5]

Being in debt is a really tough challenge to face, as millions of people have chalked it up to being a way of life and have the attitude that they will never get out from under debt. It's often one of the most embarrassing parts of life—and one that gets swept under the carpet, is never shared, and continually increases year after year behind the scenes. It is ever so important to realize that you are not alone.

The media refers to the credit card debt and student loan debt as a "crisis," "terrible news for our future," and "more debt than ever!" Let's step back and revisit 2008. In 2008, the U.S. experienced the worst financial crisis since the Great Depression. Stock markets plummeted, housing markets crashed, foreclosure rates started climbing, credit card debt reached $1.02 trillion, and the unemployment rate started to climb. In just more than a year the unemployment rate rose from 5.8% in July 2008 to a peak in October 2009 of 10% according to the Bureau of Labor Statistics.[6] Fast-forward just 10 short years, and it is apparent that this cycle is repeating itself, as individuals are racking up debt again at levels greater than the worst financial crisis in history!

Individuals are one financial hardship away from a financial disaster.

So, why are consumers repeating history and increasing debt

levels again? When you listen to or read the news the overall consensus is that consumer confidence is alive and strong, the unemployment rate is low again at 4.1%, overall job security and confidence are both good, consumers are buying new cars in record numbers, and consumer spending is good. With all this great news buzzing around, why are debt levels peaking once again?

Debt is increasing for several reasons. First of all, credit card companies have eased their guidelines and are again allowing consumers to obtain credit easily. This is resulting in individuals opening new accounts in an effort to transfer their existing debt to lower interest rates. However, once that new account gets maxed out, the old card with available credit becomes the new method for spending. This cycle keeps repeating and individuals dig deeper and deeper into debt.

Second, consumers are spending at levels that outpace their income and this is a very dangerous position to be in. Here is why: Consumer spending is rising faster than incomes support, and consumers are having to dip into their savings accounts or charge on credit cards to make ends meet. With consumer spending rising faster than wages, savings accounts for individuals are either declining or not available, forcing individuals to charge on credit cards. This is a sign that consumers are spending more than they make, resulting in individuals either having to withdraw from savings accounts to cover monthly expenses or use credit cards to cover basic living expenses. A recent article published by CNN Money reported that "half of America has *no* financial cushion" and "they have too much debt and report being stressed."[7]

Third, in addition to credit card debt, the average auto loan term and balance are also increasing. According to a recent article published by CNN Money, Americans are going deeper into debt to buy autos. According to Edmunds.com, "the average auto loan stretched to 69.3 months and the average balance was

$30,945."[8] That is the longest average loan term and amount every recorded by Edmunds, which has been tracking this data since 2002.

We live in a land of consumption and spend everything that is available versus paying down debt, saving, and living within our means. Individuals want so badly to grow and get better at everything that they do, from excelling at their career, to picking the perfect car, having the latest iPhone, eating at the new trendy restaurant, shopping the latest fashion trends, taking the best vacations—all to prove to society that they can post it on social media and not experience "FOMO" (*fear of missing out*).

But, keeping up with the Joneses, Johnsons, and Smiths is being done with a very costly price tag. Rather than feeling good about all of these fabulous purchases, Americans are becoming ill from money stress, gaining weight, and turning to alternative ways to mask the credit card debt pain.

Lastly, with student loan debt climbing annually, students are graduating with degrees and expectations of a promising career but are stressed out and struggling to pay off their debt.

Although in so many cases student loan debt is justified and clearly needed for a college education, it is a serious struggle for students when they get out of college, have to live paycheck to paycheck, and, many times, are forced to move home with Mom and Dad just to make ends meet.

It is apparent that individuals are living beyond their means and if a hardship were to occur with the loss of a job or a medical emergency, individuals would not have the savings to cover their monthly expenses.

Strong consumer spending and auto purchases at record levels are fantastic signs of a strong economic outlook, but we need to take the time to learn where the funds are coming from to boost these economic reports, learn from these experiences, and get out from under before history repeats itself and another financial crisis occurs.

If you think you are alone with being in debt, think again! All sorts of people with whom you interact daily—family, friends, colleagues, professionals—are in debt. The brave are the ones who wake up one day and say, "I am done and want to get out from under" and start living a life that provides freedom from the monthly debt statements.

The old saying that things in life never come easy is very true! And in life, you have to work hard to achieve your dreams, work harder to maintain your dreams, and work the hardest to pay for all of your dreams. More times than not, those dreams get financed and leave individuals feeling as though they will never get out from under. But the truth is, you can get out from under and no matter what kind of debt it is, there is a proven process to follow that will give you the financial freedom that you have always dreamed of having!

I have used the method in this book to eliminate debt and have helped thousands of clients in my career get out of debt by using this strategy. This book gives you more than reading material. This book includes the worksheets necessary to design and identify your payoff strategy, and to eliminate your debt one creditor at a time.

Getting into debt is easy; creditors make it super easy for *anyone* to get into debt. Take a moment and think about the retailers that provide additional discounts when you open and charge with their credit card, the endless retailers that offer 0% financing for a specific number of months, and the reward programs that allow you to earn points for merchandise purchases. Creditors lure you in and make it easy to get into debt. The hard part is getting out. It is a process that takes commitment, persistence, and true dedication. This is what I want to coach you through.

Before we jump into the book, let's look at my background, as I want you to understand that I have been right where you are and want to coach you through the process one step at a time.

In my 20s I got into credit card debt. I was ashamed, overwhelmed, living paycheck to paycheck, and struggling every single month to make ends meet. I lived with two roommates, worked two jobs, and still struggled to get out from under because I did not have a well-thought-out, written plan that I could follow and stick with. Looking back on that time, it was horrible. I ate poorly, gained weight, and felt like everyone around me lived debt-free. When I finally met a mentor, sat down, and wrote a plan, it not only helped me achieve my financial goals of reducing and paying off credit card debt, it helped attract clients that also needed financial guidance and truly helped me increase my portfolio of clients. Not only was I achieving my goal, I was helping my clients achieve their goals, which resulted in further referrals and business.

During this time, I was starting my career as a mortgage loan officer and made the realization that the vast majority of loan applications from clients were littered with debt. Desperate to gain a market edge in the industry, I attended a workshop at which the message became loud and clear: Help clients get out of debt—not just mortgage debt, but any debt at all. The message was a simple one, but 20 years ago, it was a unique one—and one that I could relate to based on personal experience. It became the message on which I built my career.

Having experienced debt personally makes it easy for me to help my clients. As a mortgage professional, let me tell you, you find out more than even spouses know about an individual's financial portfolio during a loan process. Sitting down and explaining to clients that they need to get out of debt can be an extremely difficult and embarrassing discussion to have, yet it can also be a very rewarding one. I built my mortgage career with the mindset of "I am not in the business to help people build up debt, but am here to assist clients with achieving their financial dreams of getting out of debt."

I have helped coach thousands of clients pay off credit card debt and lower their monthly expenses, which has allowed clients to purchase homes, pay down mortgage debt more efficiently, and build savings accounts for financial security.

Fast-forward another 20 years, and after many requests for this topic in print, I decided to take the time to put this plan into print. My goal is to help millions of individuals get out of debt and live the financial dreams they have always wanted—and deserve—to live. Stop paying and start living! The most important step to take is the first step. So, let's take it together.

This book is designed to help you achieve your individual goal of getting out of debt. It is time to hit the big reset button and face the facts. Whether you are striving to get out of credit card debt, auto loan debt, or student loan debt, this book will guide you and give you tips and suggestions on how to organize your financial statements, identify spending habits, cut expenses, and put a plan together to achieve your goals. In order to achieve your goal, the most important step is the one you are about to take—the first one!

Everyone has the ability to achieve this dream. You just need all of the steps to take you down the path to financial success. So, let's not delay any longer. Let's jump right into how to get your personal finances on track, teach you how to live within your budget, obtain your financial goals, and build the financial freedom that you have always dreamed of having!

Part 1

Become Your Own
Debt Detective

Chapter 1
Gather the Evidence

Learning is a matter of gathering knowledge; wisdom is applying that knowledge.

— Roopleen

With more than 25 years of experience helping clients face the daunting challenge of getting out of debt, I have seen firsthand the mental stress that accompanies debt. That mental stress often leads to physical pain in the form of headaches, insomnia, weight gain, illness (leading to missed work, which only makes the problem worse), and more. Not dealing with the pain of facing debt and continuing without a plan to pay off debt will eventually lead to larger, more serious medical issues.

When this reality hit me with many, many clients, I realized that my gift as a mortgage professional was not about helping people get deeper into debt with a mortgage, but to help clients get out of debt completely!

As a mortgage professional, I see more about a client's financial package than any other professional that works with money portfolios. At times, I often view credit accounts that significant others do not know exist and am regularly asked to "not bring attention to the credit balance."

Reviewing clients' packages has provided such amazing opportunities to teach clients financial literacy, budgeting, money management, and good spending habits. And in my opinion, providing this advice can truly only be taught by someone who has been in debt, developed a plan that worked to get out of debt, and felt the overwhelming feeling of being in debt. The best teacher is one who has lived the experience, learned from it, and can share the lesson with others.

My Evidence Story

When I was in my 20s I got into debt. Thankfully, I met a wonderful mentor, with whom I confided and shared how much debt I had. She gave me the best advice that any person has ever given me in life: to sit down, face it, write it down, post it in my house, and figure out a plan to get out from under. She had absolutely no knowledge or input on how to structure the plan but told me that based on my financial background, I could figure it out. So, I did!

I sat down, reviewed each and every credit card bill, documented my findings on paper, made several copies, and posted the evidence all around my apartment. Yes, you read that correctly: I posted them throughout my apartment. The ugly facts were on my bathroom mirror, my desk, my refrigerator, and in my daily business planner. I had to look at the facts daily to stay focused and committed to my BHAG (big, hairy, audacious goal): to get out of debt.

When a friend stopped by to visit, it felt like I was in a *Seinfeld* or *Big Bang Theory* episode. The doorbell would ring and, before I would open the door, I would run around the apartment and take down all of the papers with my debt documented. I was too embarrassed to allow anyone to see that I was in debt.

I was not proud of getting myself into debt. Not a single person is proud of debt; most are so embarrassed that it is a big secret that they hide. The reality is, most people have a "secret debt" story and it is so important to know that you are not alone. According to a December 2017 The Motley Fool, LLC article, "45.6% of households in America carry a credit card balance each year."[1] And, more than 44 million graduates have student loans according to a February 2018 *Time* article.[2] Based on those huge figures, I bet you personally know several family members, friends, colleagues, and neighbors who are in debt.

I am proud that when my mentor took the time to encourage me to face my "debt secret," I did something about it. The experience taught me how to respect money and manage money, and now I'm ready to share the necessary tools to help you achieve the same goal—and for you to feel the same pride once you take the steps necessary to achieve this goal.

Let's Gather *Your* Evidence

The most painful part of this process is facing how much debt you have and recognizing that you need to do something about it. Once you face it and develop a plan, the pain starts to go away and the bills start to shrink. It is just like going to a doctor for pain: The doctor puts you on a health plan to help get rid of the pain. The more closely you follow the plan, the faster the pain goes away. With your persistence, the payoff begins and holds many, many rewards for you! Let's get started. Here is what you need:

- One file folder
- Highlighter

Every single month bills come in and payments go out. We're like bill-paying robots. Each month individuals around the world sit down to pay their monthly stack of bills. For many, this is the most painful seat they sit in every single month. People enjoy going to the dentist more than sitting down and paying bills! People dread paying bills and wish that a miracle would magically take all of their debts away and they would never have to write a check again. Then reality sets in, the bills need to be paid, and this vicious cycle repeats every single month. You have the power to stop this cycle and make magic happen with your money.

When bills arrive in the mail or in your inbox, take the time to open the statement or the email. Please don't just rip off the payment coupon, find the amount due, write the check, and either throw the statement away, delete the email, or shred the ugly evidence that identifies just how much you really owe. Open the envelopes, print the statements, and stack each and every monthly statement that you receive in the file folder.

The file folder should include every bill that you either pay online or write a check for monthly. Statements should include mortgage or rent, auto loan(s), credit card(s), student loan(s), utilities, cable, water, insurance, cellular phone, bank statements, and any other miscellaneous statement(s) that you receive monthly. Having these statements in one folder will help to create the visuals you will need to stay focused on your goal and easily create an organized filing system (more on that in Chapter 3).

Next, pull out every credit account that you want to pay off. Once you have that stack, review each statement and circle or highlight the following pertinent information:

- Balance
- Minimum payment
- Interest rate
- Actual payment

Repeat the above with every single statement that you receive. If you do not receive a statement or have shredded the evidence, go online or call the creditor to ask for this information. You're going to use all of the information you're gathering now to complete worksheets and visuals in future chapters, so it is crucial that you highlight and save these statements.

Once you have completed the above, put all of the statements back into the folder. In the next chapter, you will need access to all of the credit account statements with the highlighted information to complete a worksheet, and in Chapter 3 you will need all of the documents to create an organized filing system.

Debt is just a pain to begin with, but why allow debt to affect your physical being and create physical pain too? Taking the first step—facing the debt—is the most crucial step in the process. And believe it or not, once you take this first step, it is easier to take the second and then the third. Before you know it you will be ready to run—run from the excessive spending, run into a debt-free future, and run to the bank to build your savings account.

Chapter 2
Document the Findings

Identify your problems, but give your power and energy to solutions.

— Tony Robbins

In Chapter 1 you collected all of your monthly statements. Using just your credit card statements and/or your student loan statements, and any additional debt that you want to pay off, let's complete the first visual activity in this book. On each statement, you should have highlighted the items needed for this form. In addition to the statements, you will need the following:

- The Facts Worksheet (see Appendix A)
- Pen
- Statements for credit cards or loans

Use The Facts Worksheet to note the name of the creditor, the balance, the interest rate, the minimum payment, and the actual payment for each and every account you wish to pay off.

The creditor is the company that issued the loan, whether it be a credit card, student loan, or any other loan. The balance is the total outstanding balance due, not the credit limit. (The balance is the amount that you owe; the credit limit is the maximum amount you can charge on the credit card.) The interest rate is the annual percentage rate that is noted on the statement. Typically, there are two rates noted: 1) the interest rate for merchandise purchases and 2) the interest rate for cash advances. If you have both, note both in the same column. There may be only one option if you have not obtained a cash advance. The minimum payment is the amount that the creditor requires you to pay monthly to avoid costly fees and the actual payment is any amount you pay above and beyond the minimum. For example, if your minimum payment is $60 per month and you pay $100 per month, note the minimum of $60 in the minimum payment column and the $100 payment in the actual payment column. Note both amounts, as this will help with your payoff plan.

Following are two sample The Facts Worksheets to help guide you through this process. The first is an example specific to an individual who has just credit card debt. The second provides an example of an individual who has student loan debt and credit card debt. Regardless of the type of debt you have (credit card, personal loan, student loan, auto loan, etc.), the following examples can be used to document the various accounts.

Example 1:

THE FACTS

Card/ Loan	Balance	Interest Rate (%)	Minimum Payment	Actual Payment
Macy's	$1,500	25.74%	$60	$100
Visa	$6,500	18.24%	$260	$300
Best Buy	$1,500	25.24%	$60	$100
Visa	$6,500	15.49%	$260	$300
Target	$1,000	23.15%	$40	$100
Total	$17,000		$680	$900

Example 2:

Card/ Loan	Balance	Interest Rate (%)	Minimum Payment	Actual Payment
THE FACTS				
Student Loan A	$10,000	6.80%	$90	$150
Student Loan B	$10,000	4.29%	$75	$150
Student Loan C	$7,500	4.66%	$60	$80
Citi Visa	$4,000	15.49%	$80	$100
Target	$500	23.15%	$15	$25
Total	$32,000		$320	$505

Congratulations! You have officially documented all of your debt. Be sure to keep The Facts Worksheet handy. You will use this information in Chapter 7, when you identify which creditor to pay off first, second, third, and so forth, until all creditors are paid off.

Next, we are going to create a filing system to organize your finances. Grab your stack of statements, and let's move on.

Chapter 3

Create an Organized Filing System

Organizing is what you do before you do something, so that when you do it, it is not all mixed up.

— A.A. Milne

Pain before pleasure. We all know that challenges in life always seem to be painful when we are in the middle of them. But, when they are over, we look back and say, "Geez, that was not so bad after all!" No matter what the task or challenge is, the first step—starting—is the most important. Procrastinating is the easiest step of all. Once you get started and get caught up in the action of doing a task, though, it gets easier and easier as you become more engrossed and committed, and you can't wait to see the outcome.

When you want to procrastinate, it is amazing what you find yourself doing. Several times while writing and editing this book, I found myself procrastinating by calling a friend, cooking a new recipe, cleaning—you name it, and I probably did it. This is completely normal. But once you get moving, you gain momentum.

This momentum can come from simple things, like cleaning out a closet, the garage, or even just a drawer. The same goes for cleaning up your financial closet or drawer. You have already started this process! You have faced the debt (COMPLETE) and gathered monthly statements and bills (COMPLETE). Now let's organize your filing system so that you can easily find the documents needed to review your spending habits and create your personal plan to get rid of the debt—so that you can enjoy the freedom of being debt free! Additionally, having your documents in order will help you stay on track for years to come and allow you to easily access documents when needed.

Once you make the commitment and the momentum gets started, it will get easier and easier. I promise you that during this journey your attitude will shift from dreading the thought of sitting down to pay bills to being excited about sitting down to pay bills. The more progress you make, the more excited you will be. At the end of the journey, you will be so grateful and thankful that you took the first step, that you will be off celebrating your new-found freedom and enjoying your life to the fullest!

Let's get started and get your financial drawer in order! Here is what you will need:

- File folders
- Pen
- File folder box/drawer
- Computer (if you prefer paperless)

First, pull out the folder with the credit account statements and bills that you gathered in Chapter 1. You will need each of these statements, along with other pertinent documents, to create folders. Following is a checklist to help guide you regarding which additional documents you will need. (A copy of this checklist is also included in Appendix B.) It also includes the items you gathered in Chapter 1 to confirm you have everything you need to have a well-organized financial drawer.

BILL PAY FOLDER CHECKLIST

☐   Rent/mortgage statement(s) (if more than one mortgage, include all statements)

☐   Auto loan statement(s)

☐   Insurance statement (auto and home)

☐   Student loan statement(s)

☐   Credit card statement(s) (for every credit card account)

☐   Electricity statement

☐   Water statement

☐   Garbage statement

☐   Cable/Internet statement

☐   Phone statement (home and cellular)

☐   Cleaning service

☐   Gardener

☐   Pool service

☐   Trust or will

☐   Legal documents (e.g., marriage certificate, birth certificates, social security cards)

☐   Miscellaneous documents

☐   _____

☐   _____

The blank lines can be used to customize your list to include any documents or statements that are not listed, such as childcare or medical bills. For each item on the list, create a file and put in the statement/document. Label each file folder, and place the folder in your filing drawer or filing box. (If you do not have a filing drawer or box, you can purchase a plastic filing box inexpensively online. If you decide to go into a store and make the purchase, be sure to stick to your plan and purchase just the filing box and/or folders.)

Be sure to add one additional folder and label it "Bills to Pay." Each and every month as bills come in, file each bill in the "Bills to Pay" folder and simply take out this folder when it's time to pay your bills. When done, file each statement in the corresponding folder.

If you prefer a paperless filing system, you can achieve the same organized filing system on your computer. Simply create a folder for each statement/document on the Bill Pay Folder Checklist and also create a "Bills to Pay" folder. Every month when the statement arrives via email or you download it, move it to the Bills to Pay folder. Once it is paid, file it in the individual folder.

Regardless of whether you use a paper filing system or an electronic filing system, having an organized filing system for your bills and documents will allow you to quickly obtain items when needed. For example, if you have ever applied for a mortgage loan or are planning to do so in the future, the lender will ask you for many of the documents listed on the Bill Pay Folder Checklist. Being able to quickly and easily access documents allows for a less-stressful experience. Additionally, having documents organized in one location allows you to track your debt-payoff progress (you will have fewer statements to file as each creditor is paid), and build your budget, which we will be doing in Part 2.

Part 2
Know Where Your Money Goes

Chapter 4
Track Spending for 30 Days

It's not your salary that makes you rich. It's your spending habits.

— Charles A. Jaffe

Debt, everyone has it! Whether it be a mortgage loan, auto loan, auto lease, credit card, or student loan, very few people have none of the above. And although some debt is good debt and some is bad, the goal is to eliminate the "bad debt" and not be beholden to credit companies anymore! People today have become too accustomed to living with debt, so my goal is to help educate you about getting used to living without debt. Get rid of that feeling that creditors have control of your paycheck and take back that control.

Too many individuals live with debt their entire lives! It starts now in high school, moves into college, and stays with you forever. Although some debt is necessary—a student loan, a mortgage, an auto loan, even some credit card debt—the biggest thing to keep in mind is to pay it off. Never allow it to continue to grow and grow and grow.

If you need to finance something, finance the amount and then work as hard as you can to pay it off. Back in the day, the G.I. generation, also known as the "Greatest Generation," lived with the motto "pay off everything, own everything free and clear, and live within your means by following a strict budget." Times have changed—and certainly not for the better. We now buy things on credit, and charge more and more and more. We don't stop to appreciate what we have; we are always charging to get to the next place in life. The point that we have failed to realize is this: If we pay off what we have, we will enjoy it even more and won't want or need the next best thing in life! We will be completely satisfied and fulfilled. Let's get you fulfilled and determine where *your* money is being spent.

It always amazes me how quickly money comes and goes. We all work so incredibly hard to earn money to enjoy life but it seems that, for many individuals, there is just never enough to accomplish all of our financial goals to live a more fulfilling lifestyle. The process of tracking expenses to understand where each and every dollar is spent on a daily and monthly basis is a huge eye-opener for many people. By documenting expenses, you can really grasp and understand where your hard-earned money is being spent on a monthly basis and easily identify where you can trim unnecessary expenses.

Little items add up to big expenses over time. In this chapter, I share apps to track expenses, as well as suggestions for how to review credit cards or bank accounts to identify expenses and how to trim various expenses to free up funds to further accelerate the pay off of credit cards. Get ready to become vividly clear on where your hard-earned cash is being spent.

Here's How You Do It

Let's first look at a few great free apps that you can download to your smartphone to start tracking expenses:

Dollarbird: Dollarbird provides a monthly calendar to track daily expenses by category (for example, groceries, eating out, fun, gifts, transportation, etc.). The app also allows you to create custom categories. If you are a huge Starbucks fan, movie-goer, or Amazon shopper, you can add a category for each and enter amounts as you spend and then, at the end of the month, see how much you spent.

Mint: From the makers of TurboTax, this app tracks finances with ease. Track what you are spending, see where you can save money (to pay off debt), stay on top of bills, view credit cards, and bank accounts. This app can help organize and pull together all of your financial documents into one online app. If you like working from your mobile device, this is the perfect app to use to organize your documents and accounts in one place. (And you will save money because you won't have to purchase file folders or a file folder box!)

You Need a Budget: Build a budget, import transactions (deposits or expenses) from your checking account, set goals and map progress, adjust when things don't go as planned, and gain control of your money.

***

These apps are merely suggestions for you to research and determine the best fit for you. Any app that tracks expenses is acceptable. I am not promoting, pitching, or receiving any financial compensation for the above suggestions; they are the most popular apps that were identified when I surveyed clients and friends.

If you are not an "app" person and prefer pen and paper, simple solution: Carry around a notebook and pen, and jot down each purchase. The key is to take the time to make a quick note each and every time that you spend money. You will be able to categorize these expenses later.

A Day in the Life of Your Wallet

Let's go through a day of spending to help understand what you should be noting.

The alarm sounds and you hit snooze a few times. Then realize you need to jump to it, get out of bed, and get moving so that you are not late for work. You rush to take a shower. If you have kids, you scramble to get them out the door, make your way through their school's car line, and start your day. If you are lucky, you made coffee and had a quick bite to eat at home before you left.

However, for many, this is not the reality. As soon as you get mobile, your first and most important stop of the day is your local coffee house (Starbucks, Peet's, or your local cup of joe retailer). Let's be honest: *Nothing* tastes better than a fresh, hot latte made at a coffee shop—and *nothing* tastes worse than the junk your employer brews in the office kitchen every single morning.

So, you order your latte with two pumps of sweetness and a triple shot and can't help but look at the lovely display of pastries calling your name. You realize your stomach is panging with hunger pains and you add a gorgeous piece of marble bread to your order. The cashier gladly wraps it up, smiles, stares at the tip jar, and requests a payment of $7 to start your day. While you are waiting in line for the barista to make that delicious and much-needed latte, complete with coffee art in the shape of a heart, note that amount in your app or notebook.

From the coffee house, you head into your office or on with your day. Before you know it, it is lunchtime. Starving again, you make a mad dash to the deli to order a sandwich, bag of chips, and bottle of water. Lunch totals $8.50. Note the lunch expense.

Let's pause for a second and do a little reality check. If this routine sounds familiar, and you buy coffee and breakfast five days per week, you are spending $35 per week. Over an entire year, that adds up to more than $1,800! Purchasing lunch out Monday through Friday adds up to $42.50 per week, or $2,210 per year. The seemingly small daily expenses (breakfast and lunch) can cause a major leak in your budget that over a one-year period can amount to $4,000! A slight alteration of eating breakfast at home and packing a lunch daily can reduce monthly expenses by more than $300. By cutting two expenses (in other words, have breakfast at home and pack a lunch), you can apply $300 to debt and start paying down rapidly. (It will be far healthier, too!)

We have only made it through lunch. Let's look at a few more examples that may pop up throughout the day.

If you (or your children) need an afternoon pick-me-up to get through the day, you may grab a candy bar, energy bar, or soda at a cost of $3. Add that up Monday through Friday, and over a year that is an additional $780.

You head into dinnertime, exhausted from either a long day at the office or a long day of chauffeuring your children from school to activities, and the last thing you want to do is cook dinner. You stop and grab takeout at the cost of $25. It is super convenient and allows time to help with homework, but if you do that three times a week you are spending $75 per week—and $3,900 over a year. Reduce that frequency to one time per week and cook the remaining nights. According to an October 2017 simpledollar.com article, Americans eat out an average of four times per week and spend an average of $232 per month on dining out.[1] Trim that by three-quarters and you could save $175 per month.

You get the gist of how to track daily spending. Let's not forget to track spending on the weekend, so let's also look at a few common spending habits to help recognize and note.

What about the Weekend?

Like to see the latest and greatest movie at the theater? Take a moment, think about the cost, and wait until the movie is available on-demand. Seeing a movie in the theater is a costly form of entertainment: The average cost for a family of four to go to the movies, each order a drink, and share two orders of popcorn is $60. Add that up over a year, and that is $720 in movie expenses (one movie a month). Opt to trim that in half or eliminate it altogether. Obtain a subscription to Netflix for as little as $7.99 per month. Not only will you save money, but you will be able to enjoy the movie in the comfort of your own home, pause for breaks, and make your own snacks. What a great way to save money and enjoy family movie nights together.

If you are a shopper and love to purchase a new outfit to be part of the latest and greatest trend, take a good inventory of your closet and see if you can get through a year without shopping. For many, this sounds like a task that cannot be accomplished. I have great news: It can be accomplished—and it is a lot easier than you think.

When my daughter was born, I took an inventory of my closet and found clothes that still had tags on them and shoes that had never been worn. Realizing this, I committed to my husband that my New Year's resolution for 2008 was not to shop for one year! He literally laughed at me and said, "I can't wait to see this!" Being the competitive person that I am, it was *game on!* I learned how to be creative with my wardrobe and did not make a personal purchase for a year. Unless it was a necessity like deodorant, I did not buy it.

If you recall, 2008 was the year of the biggest financial crisis in decades. My girlfriends joked that my New Year's resolution was horrible for the economy because stock prices were dropping due to my lack of retail therapy. If I can do this, anyone can! From that experience, and to this day, I have never gone back to my previous spending habits. Don't get me wrong: I definitely enjoy a day of retail therapy, but my attitude is completely different. When I shop now I tend to look for classic pieces that don't go out of style, watch for things to go on sale, and limit impulse purchases. While finishing the editing of this book, I stumbled upon the book *The Year of Less* by Cait Flanders. In July 2014, Cait set a goal to not shop for an entire year. I had never heard of another individual embarking on this journey so I purchased and read the book. Although our motivations were different (I did it for fun, Cait had a purpose) the concepts were the same. The book documents Cait's 12-month journey of buying only consumables, groceries, toiletries, and gas for herself.

Prior to this challenge, she paid off $30,000 in debt and lost 30 pounds in one year.[2] I highly recommend checking this book out at your local library and learning how to live with less while on your debt paydown journey.

If you see something you want to buy, think about it for a few days. If the need is still there, then purchase. If it is not, let it go. Retailers are always introducing new trends, styles, and products, so wait it out and think about whether or not you really need to make the purchase. It is perfectly fine to shop 'til you drop—as long as you don't drop to your knees from being in debt when the credit card statement arrives in the mail.

If you love to read and find yourself always purchasing books in a bookstore or on Amazon, don't give up the pleasure of reading. Just eliminate the cost associated with it and join your local library for free.

***

If you are one who does not carry cash and makes purchases using either a debit or credit card, you can easily track your monthly expenses by reviewing each statement and adding the various categories listed previously.

Tracking to get on track is about still enjoying life—just finding better, more cost-effective ways to enjoy a cup of coffee, eat lunch out, watch a great new flick, purchase a new outfit, or immerse yourself in a great new novel. The next chapter offers suggestions on additional areas to cut and trim expenses daily and monthly.

Chapter 5
Find Expenses to Trim

Beware of little expenses. A small leak will sink a great ship.
— Benjamin Franklin

Finding creative ways to reduce spending habits is a necessary step to help free up funds to pay down debt. Learning new spending habits begins with reducing existing spending habits, which will lead to long-term positive spending habits.

When it comes to reducing spending, it is no different than making the decision to lose weight. When you decide to lose weight, you reduce the amount of food you eat; you don't eliminate food altogether and starve. At first it always feels like you are starving, and then about 14 days into your new eating program you begin to see the results. The excitement of progress motivates you to keep going and sustains your commitment to complete the program.

Many individuals join gyms or hire professionals to guide them through their commitment to weight loss. My goal is to help coach each and every individual who reads this book to find the courage necessary to face their debt, identify places to trim, develop a plan to pay off debt, and then get moving down the road to a debt-free lifestyle. Here is what you need for this chapter:

- Expenses noted from Chapter 4 (notebook or phone app)
- Expenses to Trim Worksheet (Appendix C)
- Dialing for Dollar$ Worksheet (Appendix E)
- Pen
- Calculator

In this section, I provide many examples to help guide you in areas to explore when trimming your expenses. As you review your own daily and monthly spending habits, you will find additional areas that are not listed here.

From the expenses that you tracked for 30 days in Chapter 4, use the Expenses to Trim Worksheet (Appendix C) and note the expenses. If the expense is daily, use the following formula to calculate the amounts. We'll use the daily latte as an example. In the Expense column, write the name of the expense (Daily latte). Next, grab your calculator. Multiply the daily amount ($7) by 5 days per week (this number may vary; you may only drink lattes three times per week, so adjust where needed), which is $35 per week. Then, multiply $35 per week by 4 weeks in the month, which is $140. Note that amount in the Monthly Amount column.

Next, take $140 and multiply it by 12 (months per year) and note the annual amount of $1,680 in Annual Amount column. Now, decide how much you are willing to reduce the amount. Let's say you are really motivated and decide to trim the annual amount by a whopping $1,500. Take the $1,500 and divide that amount by 12. Trimming just this expense will provide $125 monthly to pay down debt. Note $125 in the Monthly Amount for Debt Paydown column. Just to recap, for daily expenses use the following formula:

- *Daily amount × number of days per week × 4 weeks = monthly amount*
- *Monthly amount × 12 months = annual amount*
- *Amount to trim annually / 12 = monthly amount for debt paydown*

Use the same formula for each monthly expense. Let's use the dining out example below. Add up each time you dined out over the course of the month. The figure totals $325. Next, multiply the monthly amount by 12 months. The annual amount is $3,900. Review that amount and decide how much you will trim the expense. Say motivation kicks in and you trim the expense by $2,000. Take the $2,000 and divide by 12. You'll save $167 monthly by cutting back on eating out. Again, let's recap. Here is the formula for calculating monthly expenses:

- *Monthly amount × 12 months = annual amount*
- *Amount to trim annually / 12 = monthly amount for debt pay down*

EXPENSES TO TRIM

Expense	Monthly Amount	Annual Amount	Trim Amount Annually	Monthly Amount for Debt Paydown
Daily latte	$140	$1,680	$1,500	$125
Movies	$60	$720	$600	$50
Dining out	$325	$3,900	$2,000	$167
Clothes shopping	$200	$2,400	$2,000	$167
Dry cleaning	$50	$600	$120	$10
Manicures/pedicures	$30	$360	$180	$15
Lunch	$185	$2,220	$1,500	$125
Afternoon snack	$65	$780	$500	$41
Housecleaner	$200	$2,400	$1,200	$100
Subscriptions	$10	$120	$60	$5
Wine clubs	$20	$240	$120	$10
Book/magazines	$30	$360	$300	$25
Apps for phone	$20	$240	$120	$10
Total	$1,335	$16,020	$10,200	$850

Using these expenses, let's look at two examples of how individuals, Sally and Tom, can use these amounts to restructure
where their money is spent each month and, rather than put it
to the expense, apply it to credit card debt.

Let's say Sally loves lattes, movies, books, and dining out. If
Sally trims lattes by $1,500 per year, movies by $600 per year,
books by $300, and dining out by $2,000, those four adjustments
will allow Sally to apply $367 to debt monthly. Trimming allows
Sally to continue to enjoy the things she loves, just not as frequently. Sally may have a latte once a month (versus five days a
week), go to the movies one time per quarter (versus monthly),
eat out less frequently, and check out books at the library instead
of buying a book online or in the bookstore.

Now, let's look at Tom. Tom likes to eat lunch out, has a
housecleaner, belongs to a wine club, and buys a lot of apps for
his iPhone. After reviewing expenses, Tom decides to pack a
lunch and trim lunch out to one time per month, have the housecleaner come every two weeks (versus weekly), and cut his wine
club membership and app purchases in half. Making these
spending adjustments allows Tom to restructure his spending
habits and pay an additional $253 per month to his debt.

Neither Sally nor Tom *eliminated* the expense; they simply
trimmed the expense. Diet, not starve; trim, not eliminate. Both
methods accomplish the goal of redirecting where your hard-
earned funds go each month, allow you to enjoy all of these
amenities, and help you work toward achieving your goal of a
debt-free future!

Other Trimmable Expenses

Other items to consider when trimming expenses include
lowering your electric bill by installing a programmable ther-
mostat or reducing your gas bill by lowering the temperature
on your water heater. Review your utility bills and determine
how much electricity you use during peak and off-peak hours.

Try to use more off-peak hours to run your dishwasher or do the laundry. Minor adjustments can reduce your overall utility bill.

Children are expensive and the older they get, the more activities they do, the higher the monthly expense for parents. Have a chat with your child(ren) and reduce activities to one sport/activity per quarter or season. Making this adjustment will save you both money and time. (And your child may actually enjoy only playing softball in the spring versus juggling between softball and swim practice.) Schedules are hectic for every parent, and eliminating one activity will reduce stress, save money on both the activity and gas, and result in a happier, calmer home.

Try to extend grooming appointments. If you typically go to the hairdresser ever four weeks, try to stretch the appointments to six weeks. Going every four weeks, you have the expense monthly, or 12 times per year. If you extend to every six weeks, you only have the expense eight times per year. That small shift can save you four haircut expenses! Let's also look at several expenses that you should review annually.

Annual Expenses

We have touched on daily expenses and weekend expenses. There are other areas to look at closely and shop around for better rates or alternative options. Let's look at a few.

Vacation: This is an annual expense that adds a large amount to credit card debt. According to a June 2017 *New York Post* article, in a study done by the financial planning company Learnvest, nearly three quarters of Americans go into debt on vacation.[1] On average, a family of four spends $4,800 per year on vacation, according to an August 2017, CreditDonkey article.[2] If you do not set up a vacation fund and budget for an annual vacation, financing this amount and making the minimum payment will be extremely costly.

For example, if you charge a $4,700 vacation at 12% interest and make the minimum payment, it will take 253 months to pay off the initial debt. Add the interest that accrued over the 253 months ($4,244) and the total cost of that vacation is now $8,944. That wonderful vacation that gave you a much-needed break will both stress you out and break your bank account. Although the initial idea sounded awesome, the end result is not worth the expense nor the overall debt incurred.

Everyone needs time off to recharge and relax. For a year or two plan a staycation and find fun things to do in your own area or backyard. Once your debt-payoff goal is met, save for the next big vacation to avoid getting into debt.

Cell phone service: Cell phone providers have been forced to reduce their monthly charges to their subscribers to keep up with the competitive marketplace. On an annual basis, take the time to call and review your cell phone statement with your provider. You may discover that you can obtain a plan at a lower rate that provides an overall better usage allowance that can save you money on a monthly basis.

Have your provider review your usage and determine if you need a larger usage plan because you are burning through your minutes and wireless data, which could add costly add-on fees. Or, review your usage to determine if your plan provides far more minutes and wireless time than needed.

Making this call annually is a must. Each year I take the time to call, and over the past two years I have saved $240 per year in cell phone bills.

Cable/Internet/telephone provider: Similar to cell phone providers, cable, Internet, and phone companies have also had to lower their monthly charges to subscribers to remain competitive. Research a bundle package that can combine your home phone, Internet, cable, and home alarm system. A bundle package provides discounts that reduce your monthly bill. Additionally, evaluate whether or not you really need a landline telephone. So many individuals use their cell phones as their primary contact number and have been able to eliminate the landline fee on a monthly basis.

When reviewing, evaluate your cable package and make certain that you are watching *all* of the channels you are paying for. If you are not a big TV buff and rarely sit down to watch a show, it may be time to pursue a more cost-effective package that provides basic cable versus a package with movie channels, sports channels, and every other trendy channel available. Having these larger networks available at the click of a button can be very expensive on a monthly basis.

Gym memberships: Fitness is extremely important on so many levels, but this is another area that can become very costly. If your fitness goal is just to jump on an elliptical, run for 30 minutes on a treadmill, and pump a few weights, you can join any gym at a relatively low membership rate and meet your fitness goal.

If your goal is to train with a trainer at CrossFit, attend a spin class, or stretch and relax at a yoga studio, take the time to track how many days per month you actually go, and make certain that the monthly fee is worth it. You may find that you can adjust your workout by walking or running outdoors (for free) and supplement spin classes, yoga classes, or strength training by purchasing a punch card for the number of days you workout. Punch cards can cost significantly less than monthly dues. Get creative with your workouts and mix them up; you will still stay in shape and potentially shed a portion of the cost!

Additionally, check your benefits package with your employer, as many large corporations pay portions of gym dues as part of their wellness programs.

Recently when talking with a client about reducing expenses, she mentioned that she was paying $200 a month for a gym membership. Being that it was a costly expense and those funds could be used to pay down debt, we came up with an alternate plan: She purchased the P90X DVD set and started working out at home. The money she was paying to the gym is now being used to pay down debt and she is able to maintain her workouts. Get creative! So many home video workouts, as well as free on-line workout tutorials and phone apps, are available at reason-able prices that you can maintain your fitness goals, stay in shape, lose a few pounds, and shed a hefty monthly gym fee.

Health insurance: Open enrollment rolls out every single year. Take the time to look at each health insurance plan being offered by your employer, and choose the best plan to cover medical expenses at the lowest monthly fee. Getting a plan under a company provides a large group discount, which can save you hundreds of dollars each month. If you have an indi-vidual plan, call the provider and review your annual cost. In-surance companies introduce new plans each year, and often the plans offer lower, more competitive rates that add up to sub-stantial savings.

Mortgage: If you have a mortgage loan, equity line of credit, or both, be sure to take the time to review each annually. There are several items to consider when considering a refinance. First, if interest rates are lower, refinancing to a lower interest rate can save you money on a monthly basis as well as save interest over the life of the loan.

Second, if you have a first mortgage and an equity line of credit or second loan, consolidating the two loans could provide a lower overall interest rate and allow for monthly savings as well as overall interest savings.

Third, if you purchased a home and put down less than 20% by obtaining a low-down-payment loan or an FHA loan, you likely have mortgage insurance and pay a fee each month to-ward mortgage insurance. If home values in your area have in-creased to a level at which you are able to either refinance or remove the mortgage insurance, it is worth doing the research.

If you have a low fixed-rate loan and have mortgage insur-ance, and the property value has increased to a level at which you owe 78% of the current value, you may be able to petition to have the mortgage insurance removed without refinancing the loan. For example, let's say you have a loan amount of $300,000, you pay mortgage insurance, and your property is now worth $385,000. Call your lender and inquire about having the mortgage insurance removed. If the loan is an FHA loan, depending when you obtained the loan, you may have to refinance to remove mortgage insurance. The guidelines have changed over the years.

Last, if you have an adjustable rate mortgage that either adjusts monthly or is fixed for five, seven, or 10 years and will eventually adjust, research fixed rate loans and consider refinancing to a fixed rate. If the rate adjusts, you could end up with a loan that provided a great low rate for several years but converts to a much higher rate with a far greater payment.

Auto loans: A quick phone call or online search will provide current interest rates for auto loans. If rates have improved since you purchased that set of wheels, it may be worth refinancing the loan. Lower rates can reduce payments and even provide options for shorter terms at the same payment, meaning the loan could be paid sooner, saving interest, payments, and money.

Home/auto insurance policies: Call your insurance provider every single year when the policy becomes due and have your agent review your policy. You may find that your mileage allowance on your car is too high, your deductible can be adjusted, or combining home and auto can make a significant difference to the overall amount you pay to your insurance provider.

Timeshare memberships: Vacations are the key to renewal and relaxation, away from the day-to-day chaotic lives that many of us lead. But, if you have a timeshare plan with any chain, take the time to see if the up-front fee, annual fee, and overall cost of the membership are really worth the price of vacation. So many great travel websites offer affordable packages that this is another expense that could be eliminated.

***

Why pay more than you need to for these services? Companies will never call you and voluntarily suggest you lower your monthly payment with a new and improved plan. You have to put in the time necessary to improve your monthly outflow. It is worth the time. Grab your statement and get on the phone right now! That phone call could save you funds needed to pay down debt. Here is a checklist of the companies to call: (This checklist is also included in Appendix D.)

Annual Review Checklist

☐   Cellular phone plan

☐   Cable/Internet/telephone plan

☐   Gym membership

☐   Health insurance plan

☐   Mortgage loan

☐   Auto loan

☐   Homeowners' insurance policy

☐   Auto insurance policy

☐   _____

☐   _____

☐   _____

☐   _____

☐   _____

Be sure to note all of the areas in which you have reduced expenses (by reviewing expenses or making phone calls) on the Dialing for Dollar$ Worksheet in Appendix E.

***

It is so important to keep in mind that tracking daily expenses and reviewing annual expenses to identify budget leaks are not meant to be tasks that make you feel like you are eliminating all of the fun from your life. They're meant to creatively find better, more cost-effective ways to still enjoy life while paying off debt and achieve your goal of a debt-free future.

There are endless ways to trim expenses to free up hard-earned cash to pay down debt. You just have to review your spending habits and get creative with your spending habits. It is not necessarily about eliminating something altogether but rather to trim to allocate funds to pay down debt.

As mentioned earlier in this chapter, opting for a staycation does not eliminate the much-needed rest, it simply allows an opportunity to save money for a few years—and explore sights in and around your area. It can also end up being far more relaxing on many levels: no packing, schlepping big suitcases, dealing with long lines at the airport, or delays and layovers, and a chance to explore activities in your own backyard.

Just recently, I was talking with a friend whose family decided to have a staycation versus traveling this summer. Their goal was to explore and take day trips to San Francisco, Napa, and Monterey. One comment she made resonated with me: The only time that they really explore the beautiful Bay Area is when they have out-of-town guests. This is true for many, including me.

Trimming small and large expenses can be rewarding, and, if you think of it as something that you can gamify, it can become fun (versus just daunting). Turn this exercise into a game and challenge yourself to see where you can trim the most and which expenses you can trim for the longest duration. For example, if you trim your latte intake, how much money can you save, for how long, and how can you replace that much-needed morning jolt? Then, if you cut the daily coffee expense for a month and apply the money you have saved to a credit card, you can reward yourself with one latte. Gamifying is all about setting goals, tracking your progress, and then getting a reward.

Loads of apps are available for your phone that allow you to set goals and chart your progress. When you achieve the goal, you get a reward. Whether you do this with an app or with a visual chart that you hang in your home, both are excellent tools that will keep you focused, motivated, and on track. Visuals are so important to achieving goals, and having a vision that you can review daily, weekly, and monthly allows you to see your progress, stay motivated, and stick with your goal. Think back to my story from Chapter 1 of having visuals all around my apartment and running around to take them down when friends came over. The visuals were a critical part of achieving my goal.

You will find that many of the expenses that you trim will remain part of your new debt-free spending plan, even when you have eliminated all of your debt. It is all a mindset—how you view your spending habits, what you really need versus want, and how focused you need to be to reach your goal to get out of debt. Programming your mind and changing the way you think about spending money are crucial to meeting your goal. In the next chapter, we detail how to shift your thinking to obtain the maximum benefit of money mindfulness.

Chapter 6
Money Mindfulness

You have to grow where you want your money to go.
— Tiffaney Malott

Once you track your spending and see where your funds are going each and every month (Chapter 4), it is far easier to trim expenses and adjust spending habits (Chapter 5). Every little bit that you shave off of spending, whether cutting down on movies, limiting dinners out at restaurants, or trimming your daily coffee habit and brewing at home, will help you focus on your goal and achieve paying off your debt sooner and more efficiently.

You have already come so far by tracking monthly expenses, getting your financial house in order, and identifying which daily, monthly, and annual expenses you can trim to achieve your goal, and you have created worksheets as visuals to keep you on track and focused. All are needed to achieve the goal, but you also have to practice "money mindfulness" to accomplish your goal. Money mindfulness includes vulnerability, patience, a clear vision on the outcome you want to achieve, changing your mindset about money, and the mental strength to stay committed. For this chapter, you will need:

• An open mind

Your mind is a very powerful tool. Used the correct way, your mind can help you achieve anything you desire. It is all about mindset; in your mind you decided you want to pay off debt. Your mind prompted the thought, you bought the book, and now you want to achieve the goal. When you set a goal, there are times that we have to practice vulnerability.

In this case, being vulnerable can mean sitting down and having a heart-to-heart with a spouse or significant other about debt that you have incurred, they have incurred, or that you incurred together. Or it can mean telling a loved one that you need to cut back on expenses and that means cutting out an activity. Having this discussion might result in the other person becoming defensive and on the attack, which could then spark emotional anger and hurt.

Initially, vulnerability may be very emotional. However, being vulnerable is also a very brave step in the process. If you recall in Chapter 1, I shared the story about being in my 20s and sharing my debt story with my mentor. That was a very vulnerable moment for me, one that was not easy, and it ended up being the most significant step I took to get out of debt. (It was the first step and it got me moving.) Once I set my mind to sharing the story and took the step to share it, it was like a 1,000-pound weight that I had been carrying had been lifted.

When we deny our stories, they define us.
When we own our stories, we get to write a brave new ending.
~ Brene Brown

Don't deny that you have debt. Set your mind and take the brave first step of being vulnerable and discussing the goal with whomever you feel is appropriate. That person may be a spouse who has been denying the story, too, or a friend who will be your cheerleader throughout the payoff journey. This is your story, so allow yourself to write a brave new ending.

This is also a time to share your plan with others, so you can avoid the temptation of giving in to the pressure of commitments or expenses that will ultimately set you back rather than push you forward. Be brave and be honest with friends and family about what you are trying to accomplish. This certainly does not mean that you have to share every single detail about debt. For example, you do not have to share how much debt you owe; you can simply say that you are committed to cutting monthly expenses, trimming debt, and living a more secure financial life.

So, when your friend calls and wants you to try the latest and greatest trendy restaurant, your colleague at work wants you to dash out and have lunch, or you feel pressure to participate in retail therapy when window shopping with a friend, be brave and tell your story. You will truly be surprised by how a friend will not only support you in your decision but may even ask for advice on how you are accomplishing this. That friend may be in the same boat and may be looking for the lifeline to the knowledge of how to "dig out" and achieve a debt-free future as well.

Think about it for a moment. Have you ever had a friend share a story about a matter that is troubling them and you were either feeling or experiencing the same story *or* had been through a similar experience and were able to offer advice and direction to that friend? It is no different when it comes to debt. Millions of people carry debt, want out of debt, and wish that they could talk with someone to gain knowledge and not be judged. It is the brave who accept where they are, have a plan to change the direction they are going, and, in the end, meet and achieve the goals that they set. True friends support and encourage friends through change; the acquaintances that do not are jealous of being left behind and too fearful to commit to making a positive change.

You will engage with both types of people, and staying mentally strong, focused, and engaged is key to achieving your goal. I can tell you firsthand that when I committed to getting out of debt and had to change my spending habits, I lost a few people that I considered friends. It was not easy, it hurt, and at times I was very lonely. However, today I acknowledge that life is better having made the commitment and choice to meet the goals that mattered to me, and the dedication to persevere was well worth the effort and the losses that were experienced along the way. Some people want you to stay where they are and don't want others to surpass or grow beyond them.

Some people will only love you as long as your fit in their box. Don't be afraid to disappoint.

~ Unknown

Patience is another mindset that you will have to practice throughout this process. It takes time to read this book, put together a well-structured plan, and pay off the debt. Keep in mind the debt was not built overnight—it likely accumulated over several years—and it will take time and patience to pay it off. The more patience you practice, the more you will accomplish, and the better the results will be for long-term success. There will be days when it will feel like you are treading water and not making progress; those are the days when you have to review your visuals and see your progress. The more frequently you look at your visual pieces, the more patience you will be able to practice.

Speaking of visuals, in addition to the worksheets in this book, consider making a vision board that you can display somewhere in your home. Part of having strong money mindfulness is maintaining a clear vision of what outcome you want to achieve and what your future will look like without debt. This is a super-fun activity. First, take the time to answer this question: What will your future look like when you are debt free? When answering this question consider the amount of money you will save each month by not having to pay creditors.

If the amount you are paying creditors is $800 per month, what will you do with the money once your debt is paid? Create a savings account? Save for a vacation? Save for a new car? Save for a down payment on a home? Whatever you decide, find images, print the images, and paste them to a poster board. Include a visual such as the Debt-o-meter (see Appendix G), Save-o-meter (see Appendix I), or Goal-o-meter (see Appendix J) thermometer so you can track where you are, the progress you are making, and where you are going. (Chapter 9 includes more details about creating a vision board.)

Set your goals based on your current situation and based on what you are ideally working toward by paying down debt. On the days when you become impatient and mentally feel like you are not getting anywhere, look at your vision board, review the progress you have made, and focus on where you are going. Shifting your mindset will help you stay motivated and focused on the goal.

Seeing the progress you make and the direction you are headed will help you change your mindset about money. This mental shift begins to happen when you pay off the first creditor and continues until you pay off the last creditor. When you review how far you have come and the mental strength it takes to reach the goal, you feel the shift in your mindset about money. You become extremely mindful about what you spend your money on and why you are spending money on various items.

After reviewing your monthly expenses and making phone calls to reduce bills, shift whatever amount you are saving monthly to paying off debt. For example, let's say you were able to trim your coffee habit by $120 per month, and you reduced your monthly cell phone bill by $20 per month, your cable and Internet bill by $30 per month, and eating out by $50 per month. You have freed up $220 per month to pay down debt. Over the course of one year that is $2,640 that you can pay toward debt. If you owe $6,000 in debt, those adjustments will have you debt free in less than three years!

All of the above-mentioned items in this chapter will help you maintain the mental strength needed to stay focused and committed to your goal. Now, it is time to start working on the plan so that *you* can experience the mental shift that comes with the money mindfulness practice. Let's put it all together and develop the plan to get the momentum going!

Part 3
Get the Momentum Going

Chapter 7

Identify Which Creditor to Pay First

People who succeed have momentum. The more they succeed, the more they want to succeed, and the more they find a way to succeed.

— Tony Robbins

N ow that you have taken the time to collect all of your monthly statements, organize your financial documents, and find ways to reduce spending and free up cash to pay down debt, it is time to create more visual charts, identify which card to pay first, and get the momentum moving. As Gretchen Rubin noted in her book *Better Than Before,* "People are not very good at tracking their expenditures; in one study when thirty people were asked to estimate the amount on their credit card bills, every person underestimated that number, by an average of almost 30 percent."[1]

You are already ahead of most! Think about your progress, so far you have:

- Organized your financial documents,
- Written down all your debt and payments,
- Tracked your spending, and
- Reviewed expenses, made calls, and reduced spending.

You are now ready to start paying off debt one card at a time! In this chapter you will need:

- The Facts Worksheet (created in Chapter 2)
- Expenses to Trim Worksheet (created in Chapter 5)
- Dialing for Dollar$ Worksheet (see Appendix E)
- Digging Down Debt Worksheet (see Appendix F)

We are going to combine figures from The Facts Worksheet, Expenses to Trim Worksheet, and Dialing for Dollar$ Worksheet, and create the Digging Down Debt worksheet.

This new worksheet will help you (1) identify which credit card to pay off first and how much additional cash you can apply to credit cards with the funds you created by trimming expenses and reducing annual costs, (2) create a visual Debt-o-meter (see Appendix G) of the total amount of debt owed, and (3) show you how to use the visuals to start chunking away at debt and stay motivated and focused. Here is an example of one of my client's credit card debts and how we restructured to pay the cards off faster:

DIGGING DOWN DEBT

Card/Loan	Balance	Interest Rate(%)	Minimum Payment	Actual Payment
Macy's	$1,500	25.74%	$60	$70
Chase Visa	$6,500	18.24%	$260	$280
Best Buy	$1,500	25.24%	$60	$90
Citi Visa	$6,500	15.49%	$260	$300
Target	$1,000	23.15%	$40	$60
Budget cutback				$100
Total	$17,000		$680	$900

Many people feel that if they pay a little extra to each credit card, as shown in this example, they will eliminate the debt quickly. However, I don't agree with this strategy at all. In order to get the momentum going and see real progress, you need to do a couple of things:

Stop spending on credit cards altogether! If you don't stop spending, regardless of how much extra you pay, the balances will continue to grow, and you will never get out from under.

A focused plan of attack is a *must!* Focus on paying off one credit card at a time. Make the minimum payment on all but one, and take the additional payments being made on all other accounts and pay it to one card. Let's restructure the previous chart:

DIGGING DOWN DEBT

Card/Loan	Balance	Interest Rate (%)	Minimum Payment	Actual Payment	Difference
Macy's	$1,500	25.74%	$60	$70	$10
Chase Visa	$6,500	18.24%	$260	$280	$20
Best Buy	$1,500	25.24%	$60	$90	$30
Citi Visa	$6,500	15.49%	$260	$300	$40
Target	$1,000	23.15%	$40	$60	$20
Budget cutback					$100
Total	$17,000		$680	$800	$220

If you make just the minimum payment on all of the accounts, and take the additional $220 and pay that to just one card at a time, the card will be paid off faster than if you spread out the additional payments over several cards.

Let's pause for a moment. Fill out the Digging Down Debt Worksheet (see Appendix F) by using The Facts Worksheet (created in Chapter 2) and the Dialing for Dollar$ Worksheet (created in Chapter 4). Note all amounts again, determine the difference payment between minimum and actual payments, and note the funds created by cutting expenses either in your budget or by making calls.

Once you have noted these figures, start with the credit card that has the lowest balance to get the momentum going and then focus on the card with the highest interest rate. This is only to get the momentum going and put the payoff in motion. (If all of the balances are similar, start with the highest interest rate first.)

Using this strategy, you would make the minimum payment on all credit cards except Target. The amount that would be paid to Target would include the minimum payment plus all of the additional funds that were being paid to other cards, and the amount from the budget cutback.

If we focus on paying off Target first and restructure the monthly payment amounts, the new plan will look like this:

DIGGING DOWN DEBT

Card/Loan	Balance	Interest Rate (%)	Minimum Payment	Actual Payment
Macy's	$1,500	25.74%	$60	$60
Chase Visa	$6,500	18.24%	$260	$260
Best Buy	$1,500	25.24%	$60	$60
Citi Visa	$6,500	15.49%	$260	$260
Target	$1,000	23.15%	$40	$260 ($40 + $220)
Total	$17,000		$680	$900

Using this strategy, the Target account would be paid off in four months.

Once the Target account is paid in full, you can take the payment of $260 (that was being made to Target) and add it to your payment on another account. I would recommend focusing on the Macy's card next, as it has the highest interest rate and a balance that will pay down quickly—and keep the momentum moving. (Best Buy also has a balance of $1,500, but the Macy's interest rate is slightly higher.)

If you are a graduate student and struggling with student loan debt or a combination of student loan debt and credit card debt, the strategy is the same. Let's take a look:

DIGGING DOWN DEBT

Card/Loan	Balance	Interest Rate (%)	Minimum Payment	Actual Payment
Student Loan A	$10,000	6.80%	$90	$150
Student Loan B	$10,000	4.29%	$75	$150
Student Loan C	$7,500	4.66%	$60	$80
Citi Visa	$4,000	15.49%	$80	$100
Target	$500	23.15%	$15	$25
Budget Cutback				$100
Total	$32,000		$320	$605

Using the same strategy as an individual with all credit cards, you have to: 1) stop spending on credit cards, and 2) focus on a plan to pay off one credit card or student loan at a time. Let's restructure the student loan example, pay the minimum to all accounts except one, and review an example of paying one card or student loan at a time:

DIGGING DOWN DEBT

Card/Loan	Balance	Interest Rate (%)	Minimum Payment	Actual Payment	Difference
Student Loan A	$10,000	6.80%	$90	$150	$60
Student Loan B	$10,000	4.29%	$75	$150	$75
Student Loan C	$7,500	4.66%	$60	$80	$20
Citi Visa	$4,000	15.49%	$80	$100	$20
Target	$500	23.15%	$15	$25	$10
Budget Cutback					$100
Total	$32,000		$320	$505	$285

If you make just the minimum payment on all accounts, take the additional $285 from the Difference column, and pay that amount to just one account at a time, the account will be paid off faster than spreading out the additional payment over several accounts. I recommend starting with the account with the lowest balance first to get the momentum started and then focus on the higher rates or balances. In this case, the first account to focus on is Target, which has a combination of the highest interest rate and lowest balance.

DIGGING DOWN DEBT

Card/Loan	Balance	Interest Rate (%)	Minimum Payment	Actual Payment
Student Loan A	$10,000	6.80%	$90	$90
Student Loan B	$10,000	4.29%	$75	$75
Student Loan C	$7,500	4.66%	$60	$60
Citi Visa	$4,000	15.49%	$80	$80
Target	$500	23.15%	$15	$300 ($15 + $285)
Total	$32,000		$320	$605

If you use this method, Target will be paid in full in two months. Once Target is paid, you can then take the $300 and add it to the minimum payment of $80 on the Visa, for a total of $380, and accelerate the payoff of the Visa account. Remember: We are striving to get the momentum started. The next chapter will focus on creating the "snowball effect," which breaks down how, each time you pay one debt off, you are building a larger payment to efficiently pay off the next account.

Let's walk through how to complete the Digging Down Debt Worksheet. Using the accounts that you noted on The Facts Worksheet, enter each account, balance, interest rate, and actual payment. If you are paying more than the minimum payment, note the difference in payment for each card. For example, if the minimum payment is $40 and you pay $60, note the $20. All of the additional payments will be added together to apply to one credit card. (Be sure to add all of the amounts that you pay in additional payments together. If you pay $20 extra to Target, $30 extra to Best Buy, and $20 extra on a student loan, the total would be $70 in additional payments.)

Next, use the List of Expenses to Trim (created in Chapter 5) and the Dialing for Dollars$ Worksheet (Appendix E). Add the total amount that you trimmed from each of these. For example, if you trimmed $100 in expenses (e.g., coffee, movies, dining out) and $60 when you called your service providers (e.g., cell phone, cable, Internet), you have $160.

Next, add the additional payments and the funds from trimming expenses together to get the additional payment that you will make to one credit card. Using the examples here, you would have $70 in additional payments plus $160 from trimming expenses, for a total of $230 that you can pay to a credit card.

Review your list of creditors and decide which account you are going to pay off first. If you have a few accounts with small balances, regardless of the interest rate, focus on one of those accounts first to get the payoff momentum going. If all of the balances are similar, start with the account with the highest interest rate. Make the minimum payment to every account *except* the card you are focusing on paying off first.

The account that you are focusing on paying off first should have a payment that includes the minimum payment **plus** the total amount of all other minimum payments **plus** the money you saved from trimming expenses and dialing for dollars. If you have a card with a minimum payment of $40 and we add the total from the savings above, you would pay the minimum payment of $40 plus $230, for a total payment of $270.

Each time you pay off an account, create a new Digging

Down Debt Worksheet and restructure the payments (more on this in the next chapter). This is a great time to add a few additional visuals to the vision board you started in Chapter 6. Use the Debt-o-meter in Appendix G to note each debt and amount of each debt. The lines on the sides are the places to note the name and amount of each account. Be sure to total the amount of all debt that you are striving to pay off and note that figure at the top—the Payoff Goal. As you pay off each account, color in the thermometer to track your progress. This will allow you to constantly see your progress and how much you have accomplished.

Visuals are all part of staying focused and keeping the momentum going. Let's move on to Chapter 8, which will help you fill that Debt-o-meter to the very top!

Chapter 8
Create the Snowball Effect

Success is like a snowball…. You gotta get it moving and the more you roll in the right direction the greater it gets.

— Steve Ferrante

Congratulations—you have paid off one creditor! Now it is time to focus on which card to pay next and create a snowball effect to *really* get the momentum going. The snowball effect is created by taking the payment that you were paying to the previous creditor (in our example from the previous chapter, Target) and adding it to the minimum payment of the next creditor that you will pay. The goal is to increase the monthly payment each time a creditor is paid off, which will decrease the debt load faster. Here is what you need for this chapter:

- Blank Digging Down Debt Worksheets (Appendix F)

When the second credit card is paid off, that payment will then be added to the payment of the third creditor. This continues until all debts are paid in full. Because the payment grows with each paid off account, it is just like building a snowball: The more you add, the bigger it gets—and, in this case, the faster the debts get paid!

With Target paid off, let's determine the next account to pay. Looking at the following, Macy's has the highest interest rate and a balance that can be paid off quickly. To create the snowball effect, take the $260 that was being paid to Target and add that to the minimum payment of $60 to Macy's, for a total payment of $320.

Digging Out

DIGGING DOWN DEBT

Card/Loan	Balance	Interest Rate (%)	Minimum Payment	Actual Payment
Macy's	$1,500	25.74%	$60	$320 ($60 + $260)
Chase Visa	$6,500	18.24%	$260	$260
Best Buy	$1,500	25.24%	$60	$60
Citi Visa	$6,500	15.49%	$260	$260
Total	$16,000		$640	$900

By applying the larger payment, the Macy's card is paid off in five months! In nine months, you have paid off two credit cards in the amount of $2,500, and you now have $320 to pay toward the next card, which should be Best Buy. To keep the snowball effect in motion, take the $320 that was being paid to Macy's and add that to the minimum payment of $60 to Best Buy, for a total payment of $380.

Chapter 8   75

DIGGING DOWN DEBT				
Card/Loan	Balance	Interest Rate (%)	Minimum Payment	Actual Payment
Chase Visa	$6,500	18.24%	$260	$260
Best Buy	$1,500	25.24%	$60	$380 ($60 + $320)
Citi Visa	$6,500	15.49%	$260	$260
Total	$14,500		$580	$900

By applying the larger payment to the Best Buy account and paying $380 per month, the Best Buy account is paid in full in five months. Let's stop and reflect for a moment. If your situation is similar to this example (and for many people, it is), you have accomplished paying off three credit cards in 14 months and reduced your overall credit card debt by $4,000! The momentum is building, so let's keep this going and keep the snowball effect in motion.

Now, take the $380 that was being paid to Best Buy and add that to the minimum payment of $260 to Chase Visa, for a total payment of $640.

DIGGING DOWN DEBT

Card/Loan	Balance	Interest Rate (%)	Minimum Payment	Actual Payment
Chase Visa	$6,500	18.24%	$260	$640 ($260 + $380)
Citi Visa	$6,500	15.49%	$260	$260
Total	$13,000		$520	$900

See how the payment builds like a snowball as each card is paid off? The payment for Chase has increased from $260 to $640. The more you pay down, the larger the payment becomes to pay off the remaining creditors.

The Chase Visa will be paid off in one year! Let's reflect on how your overall progress is going. In 26 months you have paid off $10,500 in credit card debt! That is a huge accomplishment, and you are almost done. Let's keep this snowball effect in motion and apply the additional $640 that you were paying to Chase Visa to get the maximum snowball effect. Add the $640 that was being paid to Chase Visa to the minimum payment of $260 to Citi Visa, for a total payment of $900.

DIGGING DOWN DEBT

Card/Loan	Balance	Interest Rate (%)	Minimum Payment	Actual Payment
Citi Visa	$6,500	15.49%	$260	$900 ($260 + $640)
Total	$6,500		$260	$900

Bam! In *eight months* that last card is paid in full, and you are debt-free from credit card companies! Using the snowball effect and rolling one payment to the next payment, over time, you built the last payment to $900 and paid off the account in eight months. The balance was the same as the Chase Visa (which took 12 months to pay), but the bigger the payment, the shorter the time it takes to pay off the creditor.

Using the snowball method, the pain only lasted two years and 10 months. In two years and 10 months, you paid off $17,000 in credit card debt, increased your monthly cash flow by $900 dollars, and removed the biggest wad of stress from your life. Just to put this plan into perspective, if the minimum payments noted (which were calculated at 4%) were made to all of these accounts and a plan was never put into place, it would have taken 12 years and one month to pay off that same $17,000 in debt to Target, Macy's, Best Buy, Chase Visa, and Citi Visa. The interest over that period would have been $10,456. Add that amount to the original balance, and that $17,000 in debt now equals $27,456!

Using the snowball effect, you decreased the payoff term by more than nine years and only paid $1,212 in interest. Add that interest to the original debt balance of $17,000 and the debt total is $18,212. That sure feels a lot better than $27,456! So ask yourself: Was that so bad? I am sure the answer in *no*. All the effort you make to trim expenses, maximize the amount you pay to debt, and apply the snowball effect significantly reduces the duration and the stress of having debt. In a short period of time, you can create tremendous financial freedom—freedom to build a savings account, freedom from the shackles of credit card companies, and freedom from the stress and embarrassment of having debt.

Let's dig in and apply the same method to the example with student loan debt and get the snowball effect momentum going. To create the snowball effect, take the $300 that was being paid to Target and add that to the minimum payment of $80 to Citi Visa, for a total payment of $380.

DIGGING DOWN DEBT

Card/Loan	Balance	Interest Rate (%)	Minimum Payment	Actual Payment
Student Loan A	$10,000	6.80%	$90	$90
Student Loan B	$10,000	4.29%	$75	$75
Student Loan C	$7,500	4.66%	$60	$60
Citi Visa	$4,000	15.49%	$80	$380 ($80 + $300)
Total	$31,500		$305	$605

By applying the larger payment, the Citi Visa is paid in full in 12 months. In just 14 months, you have paid off two credit cards amounting to $4,500 in debt and have an additional $380 to apply to a student loan. To keep the snowball effect in motion, take the $380 that was being paid to Citi Visa and add that to the minimum payment of $90 to Student Loan A (it has the highest interest rate), for a total payment of $470.

DIGGING DOWN DEBT

Card/Loan	Balance	Interest Rate (%)	Minimum Payment	Actual Payment
Student Loan A	$10,000	6.80%	$90	$470 ($90 + $380)
Student Loan B	$10,000	4.29%	$75	$75
Student Loan C	$7,500	4.66%	$60	$60
Total	$27,500		$225	$605

Stay completely focused and continue to make the payment of $470, and Student Loan A is paid in full in 22 months. In just three years, two credit cards have been paid in full and one student loan has been paid off, for a total of $14,500 in debt. Let's continue building the payment and keep the snowball effect in motion. Take the $470 that was being paid to Student Loan A and add that to the minimum payment of $60 to Student Loan C (highest interest rate) for a total payment of $530.

DIGGING DOWN DEBT

Card/Loan	Balance	Interest Rate (%)	Minimum Payment	Actual Payment
Student Loan B	$10,000	4.29%	$75	$75
Student Loan C	$7,500	4.66%	$60	$530 ($60 + $470)
Total	$17,500		$135	$605

In just 14 months the second student loan is paid in full. Let's recap the progress: Two credit cards are paid in full, two student loans are paid in full, total debt has been reduced from $32,000 to $10,000, and there is only *one* student loan left to pay off. The payment keeps growing, and now you have $530 to apply to the last student loan. Take the $530 that was being paid to Student Loan C and add that to the minimum payment of $75 to Student Loan B, for a total payment of $605.

DIGGING DOWN DEBT

Card/Loan	Balance	Interest Rate (%)	Minimum Payment	Actual Payment
Student Loan B	$10,000	4.29%	$75	$605 ($75 + $530)
Total	$10,000		$75	$605

The last student loan is paid off in 16 months. Remember that Student Loan A had a balance of $10,000, too, and took 22 months to pay off. The larger payment reduced the payoff by six months for the same loan amount.

To become debt-free from credit cards, student loans, and a really heavy load of stress took just five years and five months! If the snowball effect plan was not used and the minimum payment noted was paid to the credit cards, it would have taken 26 years and four months to pay off *just* the credit cards (assuming a 2% minimum payment on the credit cards). Add the interest over that time period of $6,686.79 to the original credit card debt of $4,500, and the total payoff amount would be $11,186.79. Student loan terms vary, but using the payment schedule noted in the example, it would have taken 15 years and eight months to pay off the student loan debt. Add the interest for the term in the amount of $12,212 and the total student loan debt would be $39,712. Using the snowball effect plan, the overall pay off term decreased by 20 years and nine months, and reduced the overall interest of the credit card and student loan debt from $18,898 to $1,570.

Being committed to the goal, trimming expenses, and diligently working with the snowball effect plan created a stress-free financial future with the freedom to have $605 per month to start a savings account and pay into your future.

If you receive a raise or a bonus during this time, this payoff duration can be reduced by applying the additional income to a debt. Five years comes and goes so quickly that it is well worth the time investment to dig in and focus on paying down debt early on to allow for a solid and secure financial future going forward.

Using Home Equity to Consolidate

If you own a home and have equity available, you may want to consider refinancing your existing loan and taking cash out to pay off debt or student loans. There are loan options available that allow you to take cash out, and Fannie Mae introduced a loan specifically designed to allow those with student loan debt to consolidate student loans. Let's look at two examples.

Let's say you own a home that is worth $400,000; you have an outstanding mortgage in the amount of $200,000 with an interest rate of 4.25% and a monthly principal and interest payment of $983.88; and you owe $17,000 in credit card debt, with minimum payments of $680. The total monthly mortgage and credit card payments amount to $1,663.88. If you were to refinance the mortgage and take out a new mortgage loan in the amount of $220,000 with an interest rate of 4.50% (current mortgage plus credit card debt and closing costs), the new monthly payment could be $1,114.71 (principal and interest), which would provide a monthly savings of $549.17. That is a substantial monthly savings that you can start investing in a savings account or use part of to pay down the mortgage.

Now, let's look at consolidating student loans with your equity, using the same scenario: current home worth $400,000, outstanding mortgage in the amount of $200,000 with an interest rate of 4.25%, a monthly principal and interest payment of $983.88, and you owe $32,000 in student loan debt with minimum monthly payments of $320. The total monthly mortgage and student loan payments amount to $1,303.88. If you were to refinance the mortgage and take out a new mortgage loan in the amount of $235,000 with an interest rate of 4.50% (current loan plus student loans and closing costs), the new monthly payment could be $1,190.71 (principal and interest), which would provide a monthly savings of $113.17. Multiply that by 12, and you are saving more than $1,300 per year, not including any additional payments you may be making to those loans.

Another option would be to obtain a consolidation loan by either obtaining an equity line of credit on your home or for student loans, looking at resources like SoFi that offer student loan–

consolidation products. If you decide to obtain an equity line or consolidation loan, it is still a debt and it is crucial to use the snowball effect method to pay off the loan as quickly and efficiently as possible. Don't start charging again; use the savings created to pay down the new loan or put it into a savings account.

***

Regardless of the type of debt that you want to focus on paying down, using the snowball effect will provide the plan to stick with your goal and gain the momentum needed to dig out and plant seeds for a fruitful financial future! Now that you have a plan to get out of debt, let's move on to see what's next for the new and improved financial you.

Chapter 9
Plant Your Financial Tree

Do not save what is left after spending but spend what is left after saving.

— Warren Buffett

Individuals get into debt for many reasons. Those reasons can range from spending beyond a person's means, living from paycheck to paycheck, a financial hardship such as a job loss, a medical emergency, going to college and having to finance the education, or simply just living that gets you into debt. Living life, wanting new things, and providing opportunities for your children can throw your budget off. Wanting a new car, shopping, dining out, kids and their activities, social outings, and various parties—these are all expenses that may not be planned and creep up. Regardless of how you got into debt, you are taking the necessary disciplined steps to get out and are very well starting to see the light at the end of the tunnel. This is a junction in your financial future and you have to carefully plan which way to go. It is important to pave the vision of that path while you are approaching the finish line of your debt-free race.

Planning and knowing where you want to go financially when the debt is paid are the keys to a secure financial future, and now is the time to start planting your financial tree to avoid digging back into debt. It is ever so easy to reach the goal and get sidetracked with day-to-day "wants" that can throw you off track. If we use the examples from Chapter 7 and Chapter 8, the monthly amount that would be available to spend is either $900 or $605 per month. That is a good chunk of change to spend, and it can certainly feel like found money. For many, that amount can start burning a hole in your pocket, and the natural reaction would be to spend it—maybe go and buy a new wardrobe, use the monthly amount to finance a new car, take a vacation and finance it with the intention to pay it off later, or get back to the old social life and dine out frequently. Rewards are necessary; however, you don't want to slip back into old patterns of spending or creating debt especially if an emergency arises. As you approach the finish line, start focusing on the next plan and do not allow life's distractions to get in the way. I want to teach you how to use the snowball effect to build a reserve/savings account, set goals for major purchases and future investments, and design a new vision board with goals that include a fruitful financial tree, items you want to purchase, and vacations you want to take.

Let's recap what you have done so far: You have faced debt, created an organized filing system, trimmed expenses, worked out the plan to a debt-free future, and paid down debt. Now, the new and improved financial you is ready to plant your financial tree, which will grow a secure financial future. Let's keep that momentum going! Here is what you need:

- Reserve/Savings Charts (see Appendix H)
- Save-o-meter (see Appendix I)
- Poster board

Build a Reserve/Savings Account

Let's first look at how to build a reserve/savings account. Ideally this account should be built with at least six months of income. Think about how much you take home every month (your net pay) and multiply by six. That is the amount you want to have in your reserve/savings account. Set up a separate account from your checking account (it can be at the same banking institution), and each and every month transfer the amount that you were paying to credit card debt into this account. Having these funds available will provide tremendous peace of mind, such that if money becomes tight or expenses are higher than anticipated, you have a cushion to carry you through until the next paycheck and can avoid using credit cards.

If we use the funds from Chapter 7 and Chapter 8 as an example, the monthly amount that was used to pay off credit card debt was $900 per month. Now that the debt is paid in full, $900 a month is available to put into a savings account. If you were to deposit $900 per month over the next five years at an interest rate of 1%, your savings account would grow to $56,341! Continually adding to a savings account monthly helps your savings grow, which will provide you with a tremendous peace of mind. Take a look at the following chart:

RESERVE/SAVINGS CHART

Monthly Amount	Year 1	Year 2	Year 3	Year 4	Year 5
$900	$11,767	$22,744	$33,831	$45,030	$56,341

If you have $17,000 in credit card debt and pay $900 per month to get out of debt, it will take you less time to build a savings account than it takes to pay off the debt (and most likely, less time to build the savings account than it took to rack up the credit card debt).

If you continue saving $900 for 10 years, your balance will grow to $114,624.

RESERVE/SAVINGS CHART

Monthly Amount	Year 6	Year 7	Year 8	Year 9	Year 10
$900	$67,766	$79,305	$90,960	$102,733	$114,624

The *interest*ing part (no pun intended) about growing a savings account is that the more you save, the less you want to withdraw. A savings account provides such great peace of mind that the more you save, the more you will want to save. Individuals who shift their mindset from spending to saving, and have a nice cushion in the bank, tend to think twice about spending once they start building a reserve/savings fund. Even if you only invest a portion of the money that was being used to pay off debt, it will grow beautifully for you. Let's take a look at the other example from Chapter 7 and Chapter 8 and invest the amount of $605. If that amount was saved for five years, at 1% interest, the savings account would grow to $37,842. See the following chart:

RESERVE/SAVINGS CHART

Monthly Amount	Year 1	Year 2	Year 3	Year 4	Year 5
$605	$7,904	$15,277	$22,724	$30,245	$37,842

If you continued saving $605 for 10 years at 1% interest, the account would grow to $76,989.

RESERVE/SAVINGS CHART

Monthly Amount	Year 6	Year 7	Year 8	Year 9	Year 10
$605	$45,516	$53,267	$61,095	$69,002	$76,989

Money grows so much faster and more efficiently when you are paying yourself versus paying down a high-interest credit card. Take the time to think—really think—about the fact that if you have $17,000 in debt, and stick with the snowball effect plan to pay off debt and to build a savings account, you will be debt-free and have a solid savings account in four to five years (two years and 10 months to pay off debt, and one to two years for saving money)! You really can dig out from under a pile of debt and build a savings account that will grow like a money tree. You are now in a position to plant a money tree that will be for your benefit versus paying your hard-earned money to a credit card company. With so many individuals in debt and paying high interest rates to credit card companies, savings accounts are declining with Americans.

In 2017, CNBC published an incredible study that was done by GO Banking Rates on the amount individuals have saved in a savings account. The results document that 39% of Americans have $0 dollars in a savings account; 18% have less than $1,000; 12% have between $1,000 and $4,999; 6% have between $5,000 and $9,999; and a mere 25% have more than $10,000. Based on this survey, 57% have less than $1,000 in a savings account![1] It is time to shake this percentage and rapidly focus as a society on increasing the percentage of individuals who have more than $10,000 in a savings account and in turn lower the percentage of individuals who have less than $1,000 in a savings account.

I am *not* in any way sharing this information to depress you or make you feel as though you can never break free from the status quo. Quite the opposite: I am sharing this data as a tool for you to look at the data and set goals so you're not part of this statistic. Additionally, while saving and putting funds away, take the time to have a reward system. Being out of debt is a huge reward. However, when you work that hard to get out of debt and then start focusing on a reserve/savings account, it is so important to reward yourself—but the reward cannot be charged on a credit card. A reward may be small or large, depending on your overall vision. Mini rewards along the way may include purchasing a new outfit, a day of pampering, at-

tending a sporting event, or buying a new iPhone. Many clients
have rewarded themselves with vacations after they hit various
levels in their savings plans. For example, you may decide that
once you have the debt paid off and have met your savings goal
for a year, that you are going to repurpose where the savings
funds go and save for six months so that you are able to take a
vacation, purchase a home, or buy an engagement ring. Whatever the reward, it is important to set goals and have a plan for
major purchases or investments.

Set Goals for Major Purchases and Investments

All work and no play make life pretty darn dull, and rewards
have to be in place for all of your hard work! In addition to
building a reserve/savings account, you have to set goals and
plan for major purchases and other investments. This is where
the fun really begins! These goals may include saving for a down
payment to purchase a home, planning a wonderful vacation,
saving for a new car, remodeling a kitchen, or putting your child
through college; the goals and dreams can be endless. This is
where we come full circle: Setting goals takes you right back to
the beginning, with writing your goals down, creating a plan to
save and build the amount needed to fund your goal, and de-
signing a vision board to make the dream a reality. But, this
time, rather than watching those hard-earned dollars go to expensive credit card companies, the dollars will be planted to har-
vest your dreams and goals. To put this plan into action, take
the following steps to set you goals and reach for your dreams:

Step 1: Decide what you really want to purchase (home, car,
vacation, etc.). If your goal is to become a homeowner, take the
time to determine how much home you can afford and the total
loan amount you can qualify for, what the monthly payment
will be, and how much money you need to put down based on
the various loan programs available. If your goal is to go on a
vacation, determine where you want to go and what the total

cost will be (air, hotel, transportation, meals, activities, and souvenirs). The amount for the down payment for the home or the cost of your vacation will be the amount you need to set as your savings goal.

Step 2: If you want to purchase a home, take a peek around the Internet and see what homes are available in your designated price range. Once you find a home that meets your dreams, print a picture of the house for your vision board. If you want to go on vacation, search the Internet and determine where you want to go and the best price for a vacation package, and print a picture of your dream vacation for your vision board.

Step 3: Use the Goal-o-meter in Appendix J and determine how much money you will need for down payment and closing costs, and note that at the top of the Goal-o-meter. If you are planning a vacation, note the total amount for the vacation at the top of the Goal-o-meter.

Step 4: Determine how much money you can save monthly and, based on that number, determine how long it will take for you to save the total amount needed. If the amount of time takes longer than you wish, take a look at your budget and find ways to trim expenses again to make the vision a reality faster.

Step 5: Start saving the determined amount monthly. Each month that you add to your savings account, fill up the Goal-o-meter with red ink to indicate that you are getting hotter and hotter and closer and closer to your goal. Whether the goal is to purchase a home, go on vacation, purchase a new car, remodel a room, buy a new wardrobe, or something else, this step-by-step plan can be used.

Step 6: When the funds are saved, and you are ready to find that home, go on vacation, buy the car, or whatever your goal may be, you have saved for it, so start looking to make that vision a reality.

Note: If one of your goals is to purchase a home, be sure to pay a little extra to principal once you are in your home. For example, let's say you purchase a home and have a 30-year mort-gage loan (360 months) in the amount of $300,000 with an inter-est rate of 4.25% and a monthly payment of $1,475.82. If you make one extra payment per year, you will reduce the term by 52 months (just over four years) and save $37,325 in interest! Paying extra principal can either be done monthly or by making just one extra payment a year. If you would rather budget for the extra payment monthly, simply take the payment of $1,475.82, divide by 12 to get a monthly amount of $122.99, and add that monthly amount to the monthly payment for a total of $1,598.81 ($1,475.82 + $122.99 = $1,598.81). Even when you fi-nance a major purchase, keep the mindset of paying down debt. A little goes a long way, reduces the loan term, and substantially lowers the overall interest you pay on the loan.

Once you have decided what your goals will be, researched the cost, printed and labeled the Goal-o-meter, and printed the various photos for your dreams, it is time to put these items on a vision board.

Vision Board

Building a vision board lets you see what you are working hard to accomplish and visually measure the results. Taking all of the parts in this chapter, print, fill out, and add the Reserve/Savings Charts in Appendix H to your vision board. Take the time to add a visual display that clearly notes what your account balance will be at various levels. For example, set one-year, two-year, five-year, and 10-year goals. Seeing a clear plan and the growth that will occur will provide further moti-vation to keep you focused and on track with saving.

Additionally, add any rewards and purchases that you are striving to make (vacations, cars, homes, wardrobes, electronics, etc.). Whether you are saving now or in the future, cut out pic-tures of items and paste them on your board. Make the vision board a creative tool that is unique to you and your family. Regardless how big or small your goals are, remember to always stay true to yourself. Do what feels right to you and for your family, not what looks good to everyone else. Stay true to yourself and your overall long-term financial goals. You have to live a life that is authentic to you, your spouse, and your family— what is right for *you*. It is so easy to get caught up in what the "Joneses" are doing that it makes it extremely challenging to always stay true to yourself.

A dear friend of mine once shared a saying that his father always said to him: Don't go broke trying to prove to others that you are not! That saying is such a simple reminder that keeping up with others has become a way of life. You look around, and every reality show, TV ad, magazine, website, and social media feed inject feelings that you should have more, do more, and be more. It is wonderful to have goals to strive for and make you grow, to fulfill dreams, and to accomplish milestones in life, but be sure to stretch in ways that do not change who you are or what your core values are. Please don't put yourself or your family in a position in which you live a life that is stretched beyond your means.

I am a *huge* fan of writing goals and following a plan, and I believe that everyone should dream big. As Pit Bull says in his song "Give Me Everything," "Reach for the stars and if you don't grab 'em, at least you'll fall on top of the world." Always strive to grow and achieve goals. Create vision boards with goals and quotes, and map out your future. Each December, I sit down and do an annual plan. In my closet, I have a vision board with some of my favorite quotes and goals with visual pictures of places I want to go, things I want to buy, workouts I want to do, books I want to read (or publish), and the list goes on and on. When I committed to publishing this book, my coach asked me create a vision board to chart and map my progress. It was so rewarding to visually see the progress from start to finish. I have several friends who create vision boards annually, and no two are the same. There are so many great resources available to get ideas. Take the time to visit Pinterest, Google "ideas for a vision board," or watch the great YouTube video that author Jack Canfield created about vision boards. (The link to the video is included in the Resources.) And, if you prefer to remain paperless, there are apps to create vision boards on your phone. Make your board unique, make it about you, and personalize it with items that make *you* feel good, not that look good to others. One of my very favorite quotes, which I have on a wall in my house, is:

> *Create a life that feels good on the inside—not one that just looks good on the outside.*
>
> ~ Unknown

If this feels like you, take a moment to stop and reassess. You need to live a life that is authentic to you and your family, not to others around you. It is ever so easy to get caught in the "keeping up with the Joneses" mentality. Be sure and take the time to check deep within and make certain that this is authentic to you.

When I work with clients to obtain financing for the largest investment of their lifetime, I always encourage them to obtain a mortgage that allows them to continue to live life. What is the point of purchasing a home if you live only to pay the monthly mortgage payment? Know what payment level is comfortable to you and stick to it! The same principle should be considered when it is time to purchase a new car, buy a new outfit, travel to various destinations, or even make technology purchases. The reality is, if you are living that life, re-evaluate, restructure, and move on. You want to stick to the new habits you have created and stay debt-free, not build debt again. A good question to ask yourself is this: If I lost everything tomorrow, who would I be? Would the same people stick around and be around you? Would you still be the same person, or would all of the material pieces define you? Be true to you, always!

If you have young children, teach them the concepts in this chapter as well. If they receive an allowance, earn money by babysitting or mowing a neighbor's lawn, or are old enough to get a job, take the time to teach them good spending habits, and how to set and achieve savings goals, and even guide them on creating a vision board with their personal goals and dreams.

Think about it for a moment: If your children have watched you charge purchases, they view spending as a super-easy transaction. A child has no way of understanding that the "magic plastic card" has to be paid or a parent incurs a nasty slap of interest. Children may not understand that parents have to work hard to earn enough money to pay the card balance; they truly live with the notorious mindset that "money grows on trees" or plastic cards make purchases easy.

If your child earns allowance for chores, use it as a financial learning opportunity. Have them split that money up several ways: some to savings, some to charity or church (whatever you desire), and some to what I call their "blow or goal fund." The money in this category is just for spending, whether it be a toy, candy, a fidget spinner, basketball shoes, a bike, or a Slurpee. It is their money to spend on whatever they choose. You will find that when children have to spend their own hard-earned funds on fun items, they think twice before impulse spending. Have them create a mini vision board with a photo of the item, the cost, and ideas on how they can earn enough money to buy the item.

***

Regardless of what type of goal you choose to set for yourself, take the steps in this chapter and add the goal to the vision board. Having a visual goal is a very powerful method that keeps you focused on achieving the goal. Whether you want to buy a home, a car, a boat, a new wardrobe, a new outfit, a new phone, a new computer, or new furniture, use this method. Keeping your eye on the target will motivate you to achieve the results because you will continually see your progression, and you will have a well-thought-out plan of how long it will take and how much money will be needed. When you reach the goal, it will be incredibly rewarding and exciting because you worked hard, exercised discipline, and waited for your vision to become a reality.

Part 4
Stay on Track

Chapter 10
Holidays and
Special Occasions

There's something about a holiday that isn't all about how much money you spend.

— Hilarie Burton

Holidays, birthdays, weddings, anniversaries—all are ripe opportunities to spend money. More often than not, more money is spent than one expects, and the amount adds to credit card debt. And that's only the major holidays. Add in Valentine's Day, Easter, Halloween, Mother's Day, Father's Day, Grandparent's Day, Boss Appreciation Day, and Administrative Professional's Day, and the "special occasion" shopping never ends. Over time these little fun holidays add up to pretty substantial expenses.

Let's take a look at what the average person spends.[1] According to the National Retail Federation, the amount Americans spent in 2018 on Super Bowl Sunday was $15.3 billion, or an average of $82; Valentine's Day was $19.6 billion, with an average of $143; and for Easter Americans spent $18.2 billion, or an average of $150. Holy guacamole, that is a lot of money spent on pizza, chips, chocolate, cards, and egg hunts!

In 2017, Americans spent $23.6 billion on Mother's Day, or an average of $187; and $15.5 billion on Father's Day, or an average of $135. (Based on these numbers, it is pretty clear which parent is favored in American households.)

A few other areas topping the 2017 spenders list include: Halloween at $9.1 billion, or an average of $87; Independence Day at $7.1 billion, or an average of $73; and holiday shopping with a grand total of $691.9 billion, or an average of $967! Trick or treat, I think the retailers have trained us how to celebrate with a bang and really deck the halls! Regardless of the holiday, it is pretty clear that everyone indulges and experiences spending hangovers throughout the year.

If you partake in each of these fun gift-giving moments, over one year that is an additional $1,825 that you are adding to debt—that you could be using toward paying down debt or saving. Of course, we want to show our love for our sweethearts, children, and parents, and celebrate holidays, but resisting the urge for just a few years will help you create healthy spending habits going forward.

So how do you get through the holidays, special events, and traditions that are near and dear to your heart? It is all about going back to the basics and taking the time to plan, budget, and save. At the beginning of the year, take a look at your calendar and make a list of all of the birthdays, holidays, and special events (graduations, parties your children get invited to, weddings, religious celebrations, etc.) that you foresee spending funds on. This is an easy process, and you don't need a fancy format to pull this together. Simply pull out a notebook and create columns: name, holiday/event date, amount you want to spend. (See Appendix K.)

HOLIDAY / EVENT BUDGET

Date of Event	Event/Holiday	Budget Amount for Gift(s)
Example: June 17	Mom's Birthday	$100
Example: December	Holiday Shopping	$500
Total		

Determine which you can eliminate completely and which you can trim. Then divide by 12 and put away funds each and every month. Save in advance so that you have the money available to spend and don't use a credit card.

When you are paying off debt, get creative with gifts for loved ones. For Valentine's, make cards for each of your sweethearts, versus spending an average of $4 per card. I went to Target to purchase a card for my husband, daughter, aunt, daughter's teacher, and grandparents, and the total was more than $20! That did not include the candy, goodies, and dinner. I put the cards back—and had a chat with my family about cards that end up being read and tossed in a recycling bin. We decided that rather than spending money on cards, we would make our own. (Frankly, I enjoy the handwritten cards and letters that I receive from my family far more than the sappy store-bought greeting card.)

This creativity can also be used for birthdays, Father's Day, Mother's Day, Easter, anniversaries, and any other special occasion.

For major holidays, decide the maximum that you are willing to spend and stick to the budget! Look for sales, comparison-shop online, and, for goodness' sake, stick to your list. The hardest part about holiday shopping for many is the temptation. You walk into a store to pick up one gift and walk out with several. It's the "one for them, two for me mentality," and we pass it off as "Oh, it was on sale and I can't pass up a good deal"! Yes, you can. Walk away and don't purchase anything more than what you intentionally set out to purchase.

Hosting the holidays can also get extremely expensive. Holidays are all about gathering with friends and family, and everyone loves to open their home when it is decorated beautifully to entertain. However, the food, beverages, and gifts all add up and can set you back with a serious spending hangover. Again, create a budget, stick to it, and don't waiver. Or, have others contribute and bring side dishes that complement your menu, dessert items, or even beverages. Guests *always* want to help, and it makes the occasion far less stressful and expensive when you accept that help. Additionally, it is a great way to try new dishes and have more time to enjoy with guests (versus running around preparing and putting together all of the dishes for the occasion).

For gift giving during the holidays, pull names when possible and cut down on the number of gifts you have to buy. Everyone will thank you, because everyone gets sick and tired of trying to find "just the right item" for everyone on their list. Most of the time people would rather just spend time together than exchange gifts anyway. Make homemade treats if you absolutely must give a little something to every coworker. Homemade gifts usually tend to be a favorite, and the fact that you have taken the time to make a homemade assortment of cookies, a box of fudge, or a holiday cake, goes much further than if you gave a store-bought box of candy.

For birthdays, take a friend to a simple lunch or breakfast versus a fancy dinner with cocktails and a gift. In today's highly technological world, people are craving one-on-one time with friends and family. Getting together for a chat and a casual meal is far better than any gift you can buy. Most of the time, the simplest gifts and pleasures are the most memorable.

The goal here is to keep you on track and not add to or incur credit card debt. Get creative with gift giving, party planning, and attending or throwing celebrations. You will find that events and holidays can still be enjoyed without spending more than your budget allows. Making the suggestion to draw names or eliminate gift giving will relieve a load of holiday stress and pressure, and you will find that those you exchanged with will be thrilled too! I think people are just waiting for someone to break out of old traditions and start more meaningful traditions without the gifts.

Chapter 11
Resist the Urge to Spend

Too many people spend money they haven't earned, to buy things they don't want, to impress people they don't like.
— Will Rogers

We have truly become a disposables society! Think about it: When you were a child your grandmother probably had a refrigerator that you still remember to this day. Today, consumers are constantly being exposed to the latest and greatest appliances, technologies, clothing—the list goes on and on—and individuals are feeling the pressure to toss and replace. Retailers continually send sale information via snail mail and email offers that make it convenient to click and buy, text promotional offers and sales, and even prod you on social media. Think about the last time you searched for an item on the Internet, then logged into your Facebook account and the item was conveniently being advertised in your feed.

Retailers lure you in by offering 0% financing for 12 or 18 months. According to a March 2018 article in The Spruce, refrigerators should have a life span of 13 years, an oven/range should have a life span of 14 years, a dishwasher should have a life span of nine years, and a washer and dryer should have life spans of 10–13 years.[1] Yet, every Thanksgiving you see the advertisements on TV to replace your appliances and re-carpet your house before the holidays, and then as soon as Super Bowl is on the horizon, promotions begin for the latest and greatest new TV. Yes, retailers offer zero interest for a year or more, but, as the old saying goes, "If it ain't broke, don't fix it!" Unless an appliance or technology item is broken and unrepairable, don't buy into the ads, save your money, and enjoy what you have.

Cellular phones are other items that have become disposable. Every single time Apple introduces a new and improved version, the line is wrapped around the store for days with consumers eager to get their fix of the new electronic device. Consumers set up camp and sleep in the streets just to get a new iPhone—when the one they have in their pocket works perfectly fine. It is no wonder that Apple's stock has gone from $23.005707 per share in April 2008 to $177.84 per share in April 2018. And, the stock had a 7:1 split in that ten-year span on June 9, 2014.[2] In other words, that means if you owned 1,000 shares of Apple stock before the split, after the split, you owned 7,000 shares of stock.

If you think the appliance and technology craze is outrageous, according to an August 2016 article in WebpageFXInc, the average U.S. citizen will have 43 cell phones, 35 tablets, 17 desktops, seven to 17 TVs, and 13 coffee makers in his or her 79-year life span.[3] It is shocking the amount of money people are spending on these items and how frequently they are upgrading technology.

Rather than being the cool cat who owned 43 cell phones in your lifetime, wouldn't it be a wiser choice to own 10 and invest the money you saved on the additional 33? Let's explore that for a moment. If you spend on average $500 for an iPhone, 33 iPhones would amount to $16,500. This is a conservative amount at $500, as new iPhones can cost as much as $1,000 these days. If that money was invested in Apple stock, you could own 92 shares of the stock! You still have an iPhone, but you also have a nice little chunk of change invested for the future. It is not about eliminating spending altogether, it is all about making smart spending choices. Trim, not cut; diet, not starve.

What ever happened to the days that you owned items until they quit running and were no longer repairable? As a society, we need to learn to appreciate what we have versus always wanting to have the latest and greatest trendy item.

Credit card companies and retailers are notorious for offering "sweet deals" to encourage spending and racking up debt. Think about it for a moment. Individuals get constant offers from credit card companies with a signing bonus of 10,000, 25,000, 50,000, or 100,000 miles or points just for opening a new account. The offers for airline miles are endless. Retailers reward you for spending when you reach certain levels with your purchases. You receive "notes" or "incentives" in the mail to do what? To spend more! These "rewards" are part of a vicious cycle. If you are not disciplined enough to pay off the credit card debt when it arrives in the mail, your debt will add up quickly. Here is how it works, and the theme from the retailer is absolutely brilliant.

Let's say you spend $500 to update your wardrobe. The retailer sends you a $50 incentive to spend the next time you are in the store. It is promoted as a gift certificate, and many consumers view it as free money to spend. The problem is that when most people go to the store to spend the $50 note, they end up spending far more—and adding to their existing debt.

So, let's say you go in and spend $250, minus the $50 note and add $200 to the bill. The very next month a $20 incentive arrives in the mail and you decide to go back and spend the $20—but you find this absolutely amazing shirt that you can't live without and it costs $120. You apply the $20 and add $100 to your credit card bill. Your credit card bill is now $800, and you receive another $10 incentive to spend. You get the picture. Retailers create an easy way to load up the debt and basically have you in handcuffs, because the spending never stops, which adds to additional debt, higher monthly payments, steep interest rates, and loads of stress.

There are so many incentives in the marketplace (believe me, I have used them all!): Nordstrom offers note rewards for spending; Macy's offers Plenti points; Gymboree offers Gymbucks; Visa and MasterCard offer mileage, mileage plus, and hotel rewards programs; Discover offers cash back. This list goes on and on. Unless you use all of the points wisely and pay off the debt monthly, you will get caught in the viscous spending cycle and won't be able to avoid the downward spending spiral.

You must reverse the spiral to avoid financially going down the drain. If you continually become engrossed with the reward you go down the drain in debt and the retailer grows with profits. Retailers have consumers in handcuffs, and it is time to take them off and start living a financially free lifestyle versus one indebted to retailers.

It's life, it happens, and the most important steps now are to break the spending habit, focus on paying off the debt, and then develop a spending habit that will allow you to remain debt-free, be able to take advantage of point and reward programs, and live a fulling financial life.

Author Gretchen Rubin quotes several of her readers' ideas about how they control spending in her book *Better Than Before*.[4] One reader shared: "I set a money limit before going into a store to browse." Another reader "fills up her online cart, then abandons it without making a purchase." I have definitely done that but, most of the time it is solely because I became distracted with another task and forgot to go back and make the purchase. And one other reader stated: "I shop online a lot, sometimes too much. Recently, if I see something I like, I pin it to a Pinterest board instead of buying it right away. This often satisfies the 'need' to buy the item." Think about how many recipes you have pinned to Pinterest and never cooked. If it works for recipes, it will work for shopping too. Having smart spending habits is extremely important. Here are some of my favorite spending tips:

Make a list before you enter a store and stick to the list. Whether you are shopping for a new outfit or doing your weekly grocery shopping, know what you absolutely need, and discipline yourself to stick to the list and not deviate from your plan.

Set a budget when shopping and stick to the budget. If you need a new outfit for a party or event, or a new outfit to land that great new job, set a budget of what you can afford to spend and make certain that you don't exceed your allotted amount.

Use coupons when shopping! This can save a huge chunk of money. Stores offer coupons continuously and if you can get 20% off or save $20 on $50 that you spend, why not? Take advantage of sales and using coupon offers that are available. However, if you go into a store to buy a $50 item and get $20 off, please don't shift your mindset to "Well, I have an additional $20 to spend on something else." That is the exact trap retailers want you to get caught in. Take the bonus of the $20 and put it in your savings account; it is a gift, and saving it is far better than blowing it on an item you don't really need.

Wait for items to go on sale. It never fails: You purchase that great item and walk into the store two weeks later to find it on sale for 30% off. Has this ever happened to you? Taking the approach of browsing first and buying later is such a savvy way of shopping. Walk into a store, find items you like, walk away, and think about these items for a day or two. If you still can't get the items out of your mind, go back. You may be surprised that an item is now on sale! If they are out of your size, no big deal. Have them call another store and ship it for free. If they are completely out of stock, take the attitude that it was not meant to be. There will always be another newer, trendier version, and retailers are constantly rotating merchandise. The chances of your items going on sale faster than you think is very possible given the rotation.

Think about the holidays: Christmas items are in stores now before Halloween; Valentine's Day items are on display before New Year's; Easter items are available before Valentine's Day. It is an endless cycle for retailers to turn product and update seasonal items. The same goes for clothing. Retailers stock, discount, and restock with the latest and greatest styles and seasonal items. There is always something new and improved, and many times you will pay less if you wait for the item to go on sale.

***

Resisting the urge to spend is about being creative, having the courage to walk away and cool off, and not falling into the instant gratification trap. And to further eliminate the temptation to spend, the next chapter provides ways to remove yourself from retailers' mailing lists and unsolicited offers.

Chapter 12
Remove Yourself from Mailing Lists

When we clear the physical clutter from our lives, we literally make way for inspiration and "good, orderly direction" to enter.
— Julie Cameron

If you are going on a diet, you don't meet a friend at the donut shop to chat. That makes it hard to stay focused on your goal. The same goes for spending. If you are going on a spending break, find ways to remove yourself from the temptation to spend. We are taunted, tempted, and coerced to spend on so many levels: advertisements on television, unsolicited mailers in our mailboxes, and spam emails clogging our inboxes. Retailers are constantly sending information to promote spending.

When watching TV, you see ads and commercials that tempt you to shop. Advertisers promote new outfits, new cars, dining out, going to the movies—the list is endless. You can even shop while watching TV by tuning into the home shopping channels. From the comfort of your couch you can watch, shop, and incur debt! Discipline yourself to tune out versus tuning in to TV and advertisements. Either get up and walk around when commercials come on or record your favorite shows so that you can fast-forward through the commercials. In Chapter 5 we looked at lowering the cable bill. If you can remove home shopping channels you may be able to lower the monthly bill and remove the temptation of spending.

Another great way to remove all temptation is by just saying *no* to junk mail and credit card offers that show up in your mailbox. Your mailbox is full of unsolicited temptations from catalogs full of the various seasonal updates to credit card offers. You name it, you get it, from how to update your yard every single season and give it the *Better Homes and Gardens* look to the latest fashion designs. And to help pay for all of these seasonal items, you also get bombarded with credit card offers encouraging you to open additional accounts and sink yourself into debt a bit more.

If you are fed up with filling your recycling bin on a weekly basis with all this junk mail—that you have to sort through to get to the items that really need your attention—take a few minutes and stop the mailbox pileup.

Let's start with credit card offers. The credit bureaus offer a toll-free number or website that enables you to get out of having card offers mailed to you for either five years or permanently. Take a moment now, while you are reading this chapter, to take advantage of this. You can either dial 1-888-5-OPTOUT (1-888-567-8688) or opt out at www.optoutprescreen.com. You will be prompted to provide some personal information, including your home telephone number, name, address, and social security number. All information provided is confidential and used only to process your request. (If you decide that you miss all of these annoying offers, you can simply call the same number or visit the website to be added back to the list.)

Next, let's get rid of all the junk mail. The Data and Marketing Association has a mail preference service that allows you to reduce the amount of commercial advertising mail that you receive at home for 10 years. There are several ways to have your name added to the "do not mail" list; the quickest and most efficient way is to visit www.dmachoice.org. Click on the "Get Started" tab to create an account. Fill out the required fields and pay the $2 fee. Once your account is created, go to the "Manage My Mail" link and choose which offers you would like to opt out of receiving (magazines, credit offers, donations, etc.).

Submitting the information and payment online is the quickest way to get your name removed. You can also complete a form and mail the letter along with a $3 fee to the following address:

DMAchoice
Data & Marketing Association
P.O. Box 900
Cos Cob, CT 06807

Please note that you will not stop receiving mailings from organizations that are not registered with the Association's mail preference service or companies that you do business with. For example, if you have a Macy's card, you will likely continue to receive mailings from Macy's. Doing this will significantly cut down on the amount of direct mail marketing you receive but will not eliminate it altogether. Allow approximately three months to pass, as many retailers print in advance of mailing, and the Data and Marketing Association distributes the "do not mail" list quarterly to retailers (in January, April, July, and October).

If marketing catalogs continue to show up in your mailbox, take the time to phone each of the catalog companies and ask to be removed from their mailing lists. For example, certain retail store credit cards will continue to solicit you via mail if you are a credit card holder. You will need to contact each and ask that they stop further catalog mailings.

Removing your information from these lists will not only save you a lot of time and frustration, it could also curb identity theft. Mail theft is a growing issue in many communities. Neighbors and clients of mine have dealt with mail theft and had personal mail stolen from their mailbox. Taking steps to reduce the amount of mail you receive will also reduce being a victim of identity theft.

If you give your email address to any retailer you will get

weekly or, sometimes, daily emails from them prodding you with the latest seasonal items and sales.

Removing unwanted emails that come into your in-box will remove the temptation of clicking through, browsing, and then buying. The Data and Marketing Association also has an email preference service that allows you to get out of receiving unsolicited commercial email for five years. Visit the same website for direct mailing (www.dmachoice.org), click on the "Email Opt Out Service" tab, and complete the requested fields. You can also simply unsubscribe to emails or report the emails as spam or junk; that will also significantly cut down on unwanted emails.

Another common tactic for soliciting consumers with tempting credit cards offers or vacation packages is random calls or texts to your cellular phone. Take the time to register your cellular phone number and your landline number (if you still have one) by logging on to www.donotcall.gov. This is a free service that is offered by the Federal Trade Commission.

Additionally, I highly recommend purchasing a shredder for unwanted credit card offers and any information with your name on it. Put the shredder wherever you typically sort your mail. As you sort, tear off your name and address and shred that, along with any unwanted credit card offers that contain your personal information (even name and address). You certainly do not have to shred an entire magazine—just the back or front page with personal information—and all offers with your name on them.

***

You will spend a bit of time up-front unsubscribing to unwanted emails, registering your phone numbers, removing yourself from credit card offers and direct marketing pieces, and striving to get things in order, but the time you will save by not having to sort through stacks of unwanted mail will free up hours over the course of a year to do things that you enjoy.

Additionally, it will remove the temptation to purchase new seasonal items and open new credit cards, both of which will equate to saving time and money in the long run!

Chapter 13
Credit Tips

Your credit report and credit score are two of the most vital aspects of your financial health.

— Erin Lowry

Maintaining a solid credit history and a high credit score is the gateway to obtaining competitive interest rates on credit cards, auto loans, home loans, or any type of credit that you apply for. Knowing how to maintain healthy credit scores and keep your credit secure are essential to your credit/financial portfolio.

Several factors make up credit scores. The big factors are the length of credit history, payment history, and balances. The amount of time that you have had credit plays a role in your credit score. Many times when clients pay off debt, they are anxious to close their credit accounts and remove the temptation of spending.

However, doing so can actually negatively impact your credit score. For example, let's say you have had a credit card for 10 years and it is your longest reporting card on your credit history. You just paid it in full and want to close it because the interest rate is not competitive, and you don't want to be tempted to charge. If you close that account, and your other accounts do not have as long of a credit history, you could run the risk of decreasing your credit score. It would be better to lock up the card and put it in a place that you can't easily access (versus closing the account).

Payment history is also a big factor when it comes to a credit

score: 35% of the overall score. Be sure to make payments on
time; even if you have to make just the minimum payment, don't
skip or miss payments. Having a late payment reported on
credit accounts can really damage your credit score and make it
difficult to obtain new credit when needed — and the creditor
will also add a late fee to your account. The longer you make
payments on time and avoid late payment dings to your credit,
the better and higher the credit score.

Be aware that creditors continually monitor your credit. If
you are late on one card and you have an introductory rate on a
different account, that creditor may forfeit the introductory rate
and increase it to the highest rate on that particular card. If you
are late on any credit cards, you are considered "high risk" to
creditors, and they have the ability to increase your interest rate
or decrease your available credit/credit line.

Total outstanding debt plays a large role, too, when calculat-
ing a credit score: 30% of the overall score. Having too many
credit cards with balances will lower your score. If those balances are high, it will impact the score even more. Let's say, for
example, that you have a credit card with a limit of $10,000 and
you owe $9,000. That will impact your score negatively, even if
you've made all of your payments on time. Try to keep balances
at or below 30% of the available credit. For example, it your
credit limit is $10,000, keep the balance at or below $3,000.

If your balance is close to the limit on a credit card, try to pay
the card down enough to avoid going over the limit. A good way
to accomplish this is to stop spending, but you also have to be
careful that the interest the creditor adds monthly does not exceed your limit. If you exceed the limit, you could get charged
an over-the-limit fee and reduce your credit score.

You might be reading this and thinking, "Uh oh. My balances
are all high, but I have a plan now to pay off all the credit card
debt. What should I do?" Open new cards and spread the balances over the cards? No, no, no! Opening new credit accounts

will require credit inquires, which will further lower your credit score. Stick to the plan, pay off one card at a time, and do not close the account. Remember: We are working to pay off debt and improve your financial portfolio. As each debt is paid, your credit score will automatically improve.

Security Breach/Identity Theft Tips

Security breach and *identity theft* are terms that are becoming all too familiar these days. In the last few years alone there have been security breaches with companies including Anthem (Blue Cross/Blue Shield), Equifax, and JP Morgan Chase, to name a few. Retailers have also been subjected to security breaches. Ever shopped at Sears, Kmart, Best Buy, Saks Fifth Avenue, Lord and Taylor, Under Armour, Forever 21, Gamestop; purchased an airline ticket with Delta; or eaten at Panera, Sonic, Whole Foods, or Arby's? Your data may have been compromised. According to an April 2018 *Business Insider* article, these are the companies that have faced security breaches since January 2017.[1]

If you hear or read headline news about a company that has faced a security breach and you have shopped or eaten there, or a company whose services you have utilized, what do you do? You don't go out and close all of your accounts and live in fear, but you do have to take proper measures to make certain your accounts have not been compromised. The first thing you should do is check your statements. Whether you paid with a credit card or debit card, research to see if any unfamiliar charges or debits have been made. If they have, immediately call and report the fraudulent charges. The credit card company or bank will research the charge(s), handle the dispute, and likely issue a new card.

Next, depending on how severely your data has been compromised, it is a good idea to either set up a credit-monitoring service or potentially lock your credit with a security freeze/credit freeze. Among the available credit-monitoring services are LifeLock, AllClear ID, and Identity Guard. Many times, companies that have experienced a breach offer free credit monitoring to customers who may have been impacted for a specified period of time. The great thing about having a credit-monitoring company is that any time an inquiry is made for a new account, you get an alert, which keeps you on top of any suspicious activity.

If you decide that you want to place a security freeze on your credit, you have to contact each of the three major credit bureaus (Equifax, Experian, and Transunion) and request that this be done. Here's how to contact the three credit bureaus:

Equifax
PO Box 105783
Atlanta, GA 30348
1-800-685-5000
www.equifax.com

Experian National Consumer Asssitance Center
PO Box 2002
Allen, TX, 75013
1-888-397-3742
www.experian.com

Transunion Consumer Relations
P.O Box 1000
Chester, PA 19022
1-800-916-8800
www.transunion.com

A security freeze will prevent any inquiries from being made on your account. However, it is important to know that any time you need to apply for new credit, whether it be a credit card, line of credit, auto loan, or mortgage loan, you will have to contact each of the three bureaus and request that the credit be temporarily unlocked for a specific period of time. Having a security freeze in place can cause delays when obtaining new financing.

Be sure to obtain a free copy of your credit report annually and monitor it for accuracy. The one and only website to order a free credit report is www.annualcreditreport.com. The website will allow you either order one report per year with your credit data from each of the three bureaus *or* allow you to order a report with only one bureau at a time. If you choose the latter option—to order a report from just one bureau at a time—you can actually order three separate reports (one from each of the bureaus) and spread it out over a year. For example, you could order a report in January and only request your data from Experian. A few months later, in May, you could go back to annualcreditreport.com and order a report from just TransUnion. In September, you could order another credit report from just Equifax. This allows you to monitor your credit three times a year versus just once.

Whether you choose to order your report one time a year or spread it out, be sure to obtain a copy annually. Review each line item and look for any suspicious activity. Suspicious activity can be inquires that you do not recall making, accounts that you do not recognize, or even an address where you have never lived.

Also review to make sure that payments have been reported correctly. Creditors can make mistakes, and mistakes that are not caught can be costly to your credit score. Look at each of your account lines, also known as "trade lines," and review the balance, credit limit, and payment history. If you see an account that has a late reported and you do not recall ever being late, call the creditor and dispute the late payment. Having a late re-moved can significantly increase your credit score (depending on the age of the late).

Lastly, always be sure to read the fine print when you apply for or obtain new credit. Many credit card companies offer zero-interest accounts. Zero percent is a very attractive offer, but that rate is usually for a specified period of time. If you purchase an item or transfer a balance and do not pay the amount off during the introductory rate period, the creditor will automatically in-crease the interest rate, without warning, and you will get hit with a hefty interest rate and pay interest on the purchase or transfer.

***

You have worked hard to build your credit history and it is ever so important to maintain it. By paying down debt, making payments on time, keeping your credit scores high, and contin-ually monitoring your credit, you will maintain and continue to build a solid credit history.

Having a solid credit history will help you build a healthy fi-nancial portfolio, as it will provide opportunities to obtain com-petitive interest rates when borrowing money is necessary.

Conclusion

You have worked so incredibly hard to face debt, organize your finances, cut spending, pay off debt, and build vision boards. Now you get to start working toward fruitful and fulling goals that you have dreamed of achieving. If a setback happens, never lose hope; just hit the reset button, grab this book, and work back through each step. Life happens and things happen, so take the time to learn from setbacks and put a new plan together.

Our hope and goal as parents is to always make our children be better than we are, and parents never want to watch their children suffer financially. Take the time to instill good spending habits in your children. If you have children in college, send them a copy of this book and give them the gift of financial knowledge so that they can avoid getting into debt either in college or after. If they have student loans (and sometimes that is the only option), pass along a copy so they have a plan that they can put into practice as soon as they land that amazing career! If you have friends, family members, or colleagues who share their story, please share mine.

I commend you for being brave enough to pick up this book, taking the time to read this book, and working so diligently to meet your goals. I wish you an amazing journey on your new and improved financial you! We started this journey with a quote from Tony Robbins: *If you want to be successful, find someone who has achieved the results you want and copy what they do and you'll achieve the same results.*

As we close, I hope you will always remember:

Each financial path is unique and personal. Take the steps to pave your own journey!

Appendix A
Facts Worksheet

THE FACTS				
Card/ Loan	Balance	Interest Rate (%)	Minimum Payment	Actual Payment
Total				

Appendix B

BILL PAY FOLDER CHECKLIST

- ☐ Rent/mortgage statement(s) (if more than one mortgage, include all statements)
- ☐ Auto loan statement(s)
- ☐ Insurance statement (auto and home)
- ☐ Student loan statement(s)
- ☐ Credit card statement(s) (for every credit card account)
- ☐ Electricity statement
- ☐ Water statement
- ☐ Garbage statement
- ☐ Cable/Internet statement
- ☐ Phone statement (home and cellular)
- ☐ Cleaning service
- ☐ Gardener
- ☐ Pool service
- ☐ Trust or will
- ☐ Legal documents (e.g., marriage certificate, birth certificates, social security cards)
- ☐ Miscellaneous documents
- ☐ _____
- ☐ _____

Appendix C

EXPENSES TO TRIM				
Expenses	Monthly Amount	Annual Amount	Trim Amount Annually	Monthly Amount for Debt Paydown
Example: Daily Latte	$140	$1,680	$1,500	$125
Total				

Appendix D

Annual Review Checklist

- ☐ Cellular phone plan

- ☐ Cable/Internet/telephone plan

- ☐ Gym membership

- ☐ Health insurance plan

- ☐ Mortgage loan

- ☐ Auto loan

- ☐ Homeowners' insurance policy

- ☐ Auto insurance policy

- ☐ _____

- ☐ _____

- ☐ _____

- ☐ _____

- ☐ _____

Appendix E

DIALING FOR DOLLAR$

Service Provider	Current Bill	New Bill	Savings
Example: Cell Phone	$150	$120	$30
Total			

Appendix F

DIGGING DOWN DEBT

Card/ Loan	Balance	Interest Rate (%)	Minimum Payment	Actual Payment
Total				

Appendix G

Debt-o-meter

Payoff Goal

$ _____

$ _____

$ _____

$ _____

$ _____

$ _____

$ _____

$ _____

$ _____

$ _____

$ _____

$ _____

Appendix H

RESERVE/SAVINGS CHART					
Monthly Amount	Year 1	Year 2	Year 3	Year 4	Year 5

RESERVE/SAVINGS CHART					
Monthly Amount	Year 6	Year 7	Year 8	Year 9	Year 10

Appendix I

Save-o-meter

Savings Goal

$ _____

$ _____

$ _____

$ _____

$ _____

$ _____

$ _____

$ _____

$ _____

$ _____

$ _____

Goal-o-meter

_____ Goal

$ _____

$ _____

$ _____

$ _____

$ _____

$ _____

$ _____

$ _____

$ _____

$ _____

$ _____

$ _____

Appendix K

HOLIDAY / EVENT BUDGET

Date of Event	Event/Holiday	Budget Amount for Gift(s)
Example: June 17	Mom's Birthday	$100
Example: December	Holiday Shopping	$500
Total		

Chapter Notes

Introduction

1. Paul Davidson. "Credit Card Debt Hits New Record, Raising Warning Sign." *USA Today*, January 8, 2018. www.usatoday.com/story/money/2018/01/08/credit-card-debt-hits-new-record-raising-warning-sign/1014921001/.

2. Kaitlin Mulhere. "A Shocking Number of Americans Now Owe at Least $50,000 in Student Debt—and Many Aren't Paying it Down." Time.com, February 22, 2018. http://time.com/money/5169145/50000-dollars-student-debt-default/.

3. "How Much Is a Trillion?" National Public Radio transcript. Ira Flatow, host. February 8, 2008. www.npr.org/templates/transcript/transcript.php?storyId=18801012.

4. Alina Comoreanu. "Credit Card Debt Study: Trends & Insights." Wallethub.com, March 8, 2018. https://wallethub.com/edu/credit-card-debt-study/24400/.

5. Drew Cloud. "Student Loan Debt Statistics 2018." StudentLoans.net, March 21, 2018. https://studentloans.net/student-loan-debt-statistics/.

6. "Labor Force Statistics from the Current Population Survey." United States Department of Labor Bureau of Labor Statistics.
https://data.bls.gov/timeseries/LNS14000000.

7. Anna Bahney. "Half of Americans Are Spending Their Entire Paycheck (or More)." CNN Money, June 27, 2017.
http://money.cnn.com/2017/06/27/pf/expenses/index.html.

8. Peter Valdes-Dapena. "Americans Are Going Deeper into Debt to Buy Cars." CNN Money, July 4, 2017.
http://money.cnn.com/2017/07/03/autos/long-auto-loans/index.html

Chapter 1
1. Matthew Frankel. "Here's the Average American Household's Credit Card Debt—How Do You Compare?" The Motley Fool, December 11, 2017.
www.fool.com/credit-cards/2017/12/11/heres-the-average-american-households-credit-car-2.aspx.

2. Mulhere. "A Shocking Number."

Chapter 4
1. Trent Hamm. "Don't Eat Out as Often (188/365)." The Simple Dollar, October 18, 2017.
www.thesimpledollar.com/dont-eat-out-as-often-188365/.

2. Cait Flanders. *The Year of Less: How I Stopped Shopping, Gave Away My Belongings, and Discovered Life Is Worth More than Anything You Can Buy in a Store.* Hay House, 2018.

Chapter 5

1. Jacob Passy. "Most Americans Will Go into Debt to Pay for a Vacation." *New York Post,* June 21, 2017. https://nypost.com/2017/06/21/most-americans-will-go-into-debt-to-pay-for-a-vacation/.

2. Kim Pinnelli. "Study: Average Cost of a Vacation." Credit-Donkey, August 23, 2017. www.creditdonkey.com/average-cost-vacation.html.

Chapter 7

1. Gretchen Rubin. *Better Than Before.* 2015.

Chapter 9

1. Kathleen Elkins. "Here's How Much Money Americans Have in Their Savings Accounts." CNBC, September 13, 2017. www.cnbc.com/2017/09/13/how-much-americans-at-have-in-their-savings-accounts.html.

Chapter 10

1. All amounts in this section are from "Holiday Headquarters." National Retail Federation. https://nrf.com/resources/consumer-research-and-data/holiday-spending/holiday-headquarters.

Chapter 11

1. June Lawrence. "The Life Expectancy of Major Household Appliances." The Spruce, March 1, 2018. www.thespruce.com/lifespan-of-household-appliances-4158782.

2. www.nasdaq.com/symbol/aapl/stock-chart?intraday=off&timeframe=10y&charttype=ohlc&splits=on&earnings=off&movingaverage=None&lowerstudy=volume&comparison=off&index=&drilldown=off&sDefault=true.

3. Chris Zook. "How Many Devices Will You Use in Your Life?" (infographic). WebpageFXInc, August 1, 2016. www.webpagefx.com/blog/general/how-many-devices-will-you-use-in-your-life/.

4. Rubin. *Better Than Before*, pp. 207–208.

Chapter 13
1. Dennis Green. "If You Shopped at These 14 Stores in the Last Year, Your Data Might Have Been Stolen." *Business Insider*, April 6, 2018. www.businessinsider.com/data-breaches-2018-4.

Resources

Books

Better Than Before: What I Learned About Making and Breaking Habits—to Sleep More, Quit Sugar, Procrastinate Less, and Generally Build a Happier Life by Gretchen Rubin

Daring Greatly: How the Courage to Be Vulnerable Transforms the Way We Live, Love, Parent, and Lead by Brené Brown

The Year of Less: How I Stopped Shopping, Gave Away My Belongings, and Discovered Life Is Worth More Than Anything You Can Buy in a Store by Cait Flanders

Credit

Contact Information for Credit Bureaus

Equifax
PO Box 105783
Atlanta, GA 30348
1-800-685-5000
www.equifax.com

Experian National Consumer Asssitance Center
PO Box 2002
Allen, TX, 75013
1-888-397-3742
www.experian.com

Transunion Consumer Relations
P.O Box 1000
Chester, PA 19022
1-800-916-8800
www.transunion.com

Credit Card Calculator
https://www.bankrate.com/calculators/managing-debt/minimum-payment-calculator.aspx

Free Annual Credit Report
www.annualcreditreport.com
Removal from Mailing Lists

Credit Card Offers
888-5-OPTOUT (888-567-8688)
www.optoutprescreen.com

Direct Mail Offers
www.dmachoice.org

DMA choice
Data & Marketing Association
PO Box 900
Cos Cob, CT 06807

Phone Calls or Text Messages
www.donotcall.gov

Vision Board
https://www.youtube.com/watch?v=iamZEW0x3dM
https://www.pinterest.com/
https://www.huffingtonpost.com/elizabeth-rider/the-scientific-reason-why_b_6392274.html

Generations

2001 to present: New Silent Generation or Generation Z
1980 to 2000: Millennials or Generation Y
1965 to 1979: Thirteeners or Generation X
1946 to 1964: Baby Boomers
1925 to 1945: Silent Generation
1901 to 1924: G.I. Generation

Note: The above dates are approximate. Various sources and websites note dates that overlap and vary slightly.

About the Author

Jodee Brydges is a loan officer in Northern California, a national speaker/trainer, and a contributing writer for publications, and has been a guest speaker on both media and radio. She has spent the past 25 years coaching her clients, colleagues, and employees of corporations on how to transform and improve their financial health by providing the tools and knowledge needed to help individuals get out of debt, improve their overall financial health and build a secure financial future. Jodee lives in Northern California with her husband, Robert, daughter, Chloe, and wonderful Westie, Winston.

ABOOKS

ALIVE Book Publishing and ALIVE Publishing Group
are imprints of Advanced Publishing LLC,
3200 A Danville Blvd., Suite 204, Alamo, California 94507

Telephone: 925.837.7303 Fax: 925.837.6951
www.alivebookpublishing.com

www.ingramcontent.com/pod-product-compliance
Lightning Source LLC
Chambersburg PA
CBHW021113090426
42738CB00006B/622